Kindle Fire HD Tips, Tricks, and Traps:

A How-To Tutorial for the Kindle Fire HD

Edward Jones

Revised (print) edition publication date October 10, 2013
Digital rights provided by agreement to
Amazon Digital Services, Inc.
Print rights provided by agreement to
CreateSpace, an Amazon company

Other Books by Edward Jones

Top 300 Free Apps for the Kindle Fire is your guide to 300 of the top rated apps that you'll find useful for your Kindle Fire. Jones has taken the time to research and compile this extensive list of apps for your Kindle Fire, and best of all, each of these apps are FREE. You'll find apps for the home office, for entertainment, for news, weather, and sports, for your health, for managing your finances, for playing games, and more. A local news apps section provides news, weather, and traffic apps for over 50 major US cities, and a travel section gives you an insight to the best apps that will help you find great deals on flights, hotel rooms, cruises, dining, and even the best gas prices around your hometown or when on the road. Each listing begins with a clickable link back to the Amazon catalog. So as you read this book on your Kindle, if any particular app sounds like what you've been looking for, just tap the image or heading name. You'll be taken directly to the Amazon page for the app, where you can click the button to install that app. (Active wi-fi connection required.) Let Top 300 Free Apps for the Kindle Fire be your guide to the best free apps for your new tablet! (To preview this book electronicallly, go to www.amazon.com and search for the Kindle e-book "Top 300 Free Apps for the Kindle Fire."

INTRODUCTION

So, you've got a Kindle Fire as a gift, or perhaps you bit the purchase bullet on your own because you wanted this awesome tablet. However you came into possession of your Kindle Fire, you probably have unanswered questions about its operation, or would just love to get the most out of your new tablet. In this comprehensive guide, you'll learn tips (ways to effectively use your Kindle Fire), tricks (ways to improve the operation of your Kindle Fire), and traps (things to avoid to prevent problems while using your Kindle Fire). You will learn-

- How to get around to the user interface, the home screen, and the carousel more efficiently
- How to make your Kindle Fire your own, customizing its display and operation for fastest and easiest use
- How to find THOUSANDS of FREE as in, 'zero dollars and zero cents') books
- How to use the built-in camera to take photos and videos (**applies to 1st generation Fire HD and 2nd-generation 8.9-inch model ONLY; see important note below**)
- How to setup the security options to protect your account information
- How you can move your iTunes or other music library to your Kindle Fire
- How you can download YouTube videos to your Kindle Fire
- Suggested apps that no Kindle Fire owner should be without

You will learn all of the above and more, with *Kindle Fire Tips, Tricks, and Traps: A How-To Tutorial for the Kindle Fire HD* as a part of your library. Read on, and learn 100% of what you need to know to get the most out of your Kindle Fire HD!

IMPORTANT NOTE: This book covers BOTH the "second generation" Kindle Fire HD (shipping since early October 2013), and the "first generation" Kindle Fire HD (introduced in September 2012 and shipped from October 2012 through early October 2013). You can identify your generation of Kindle Fire HD by locating the volume and power off/on buttons. If these buttons lie along a beveled edge on the rear of the unit with the power button on one side and the volume buttons on the other side, you have a second generation Kindle Fire HD. If these buttons are located flush on the side of the unit with both the power and volume buttons on the same side, you have a first generation Kindle Fire HD. We note the differences where necessary.

Table of Contents

INTRODUCTION..3
Chapter 1: Kindle Fire Out of the Box...............................9
  About the Kindle Fire HD...10
  Which generation of Fire HD do I own?.....................11
  About tablet computers 11
  Where's My Data? (Fire HD Storage & the Amazon Cloud).12
  History of the Kindle Fire HD....................................16
  Setting up your Kindle Fire..18
  Controls and Layout, 2nd-Generation Kindle Fire HD..........19
  Controls and Layout, 1st-Generation Kindle Fire HD 20
Chapter 2: User-Interface Tips, Tricks, and Traps..................27
  About the Home Screen, Navigation Bar, Carousel, and
  Favorites..27
  Setting your Display...30
  Customizing your Favorites 32
  Changing Basic Settings on your Kindle Fire 33
  General Typing and Text-Entry Tips 39
Chapter 3: Free Books, Movies, and Music Tips, Tricks and
Traps...43
  Getting Kindle Books from your local library 43
  Using the Kindle Owner's Lending Library ("KOLL") to your
  advantage...45
  Easily Search the Kindle Store on your Fire for Free Books ..45
Chapter 4: Silk browser tips, tricks, and traps.....................49
  Surfing the Web with the Silk Browser 49
  Using Bookmarks...52
  Changing Silk Settings for Best Operation 53
Chapter 5: File Management Tips, Tricks, and Traps..............59
  Sending Files to your Kindle Fire via E-mail 60
  Moving Files to your Fire HD with your USB Cable 63
  Move Files Wirelessly with the Wi-Fi File Explorer App 65
Chapter 6: Email Tips, Tricks, and Traps 67
  Setting up your Kindle Fire HD E-mail 67
  Setting up E-mail with Microsoft Exchange 71
  Customize E-mail operations with various settings 73

Chapter 7: Multimedia Tips, Tricks, and Traps 77
  Playing personal videos on your Kindle Fire HD 77
  Import your iTunes/Zune Music Library to your Fire HD......80
  Downloading and playing YouTube videos............................80
  Storing pictures and personal videos in the Amazon
  CloudDrive 81
  Viewing your CloudDrive photos on a Kindle Fire 83
Chapter 8: Camera Tips, Tricks, and Traps...............................85
  Using the 1st-Gen. Kindle Fire's built-in Camera app...........86
  Adding capabilities with third-party camera apps.................89
  Changing your Camera Settings (When Necessary) 91
  Getting photos from your Fire HD to your computer 93
Chapter 9: Apps Tips, Tricks, and Traps...................................95
  About Apps 95
  Deleting Apps...96
  Troubleshooting Apps 98
  Twenty FREE Apps No Fire HD Should Be Without 100
  Crackle 101
  Netflix...102
  IMDb 103
  USA Today..104
  ESPN ScoreCenter 106
  Facebook by Facebook...107
  Calculator Plus FREE by Digital Cherry, LLC....................108
  PageOnce Money and Bills by PageOnce Corp....................109
  Checkbook...110
  HotelTonight 111
  Kayak 112
  CruiseFinder 113
  YP Local Search and Gas Prices (Kindle tablet edition).......114
  Adobe Reader by Adobe Systems 115
  iTranslate by Sonico Mobile 116
  My Alarm Clock Free (by Apalon) 118
  Inkpad Notepad for Notes (by Workpail)..............................119
  WebMD by WebMD 120
  File Manager (by Appsolutely) 121
  Wi-Fi File Explorer by Dooblou 122
Chapter 10: Printing from your Kindle Fire HD 125

Chapter 11: Security Tips, Tricks, and Traps............................129
Chapter 12: Battery and Power Tips, Tricks, and Traps 133
CONCLUSION 137

Chapter 1: Kindle Fire Out of the Box

Welcome to *Kindle Fire Tips, Tricks, and Traps: A How-To Tutorial for the Kindle Fire HD*. This is a user's guide, written to get beginners up to speed quickly, as well as to provide content that will also appeal to the more technically-savvy. In this book, you will find all the basic tips you need to quickly learn to use your Kindle Fire HD like a seasoned pro. And the more advanced topics covered in this book will help you take your use of the Kindle Fire HD to a higher level, getting the most out of your new tablet.

This book looks at three categories in every chapter: ***tips***, ***tricks***, and ***traps***.

Tips are techniques that make things easier in terms of use, in a particular area.

Tricks are techniques that change the operation of your Kindle Fire in a particular area, often providing capabilities or performance improvements that just were not there out of the box.

Traps are "gotchas," things to watch out for, that can cause problems.

About the Kindle Fire HD

The Kindle Fire HD is one product in a line of products known as Amazon Kindles. Kindles are handheld devices, designed and sold by Amazon, that let you shop for and download e-books, magazines, and other digital content using wireless technology. The Kindle Fire HD was released in September 2012, just one year after the release of the original Kindle Fire. The Kindle Fire HD is available with screens in two sizes, a 7 inch display or an 8.9 inch display, and sports stereo speakers with Dolby sound, quite an accomplishment for a device with prices starting at under $140 US at the time of this writing. Roughly one year after its initial release, in September 2013,

Amazon released new models within the Kindle Fire family: the Kindle Fire HDX, in both 7-inch and 8.9-inch (diagonal measurement) screen sizes.

It's important to note that there are, in effect, two variations of the Kindle Fire HD: those devices shipped before early October 2013, and the devices shipped since October 2013. In September of 2013, Amazon announced a reengineered Kindle Fire HD 7-inch screen model with a price reduced to $139 U.S. As part of the re-engineering, Amazon removed the front facing camera and the HDMI port, sped up the processor, relocated the volume and power off / on buttons making these easier to use, and made a major upgrade to the operating system. If you purchased your Kindle Fire new from Amazon or from a retailer after early October 2013, you likely possess the second generation Kindle Fire, covered in detail in this book (along with the first generation model). However, if you purchased your Kindle Fire prior to October 2013, or if you purchased your Kindle Fire on the used market, you'll likely have a first generation Kindle Fire HD.

Which generation of Fire HD do I own?

One easy way to tell the difference is to examine your device and locate the volume and power off / on buttons. If these buttons lie along a beveled edge on the rear of the device with the power button on one side and the volume buttons on the other side, you have a second generation Kindle Fire HD. If these buttons are located flush on the side of the device with both the power and volume buttons on the same side, you have a first generation Kindle Fire HD. Throughout this book differences in the two models will be pointed out where necessary.

About tablet computers

The Kindle Fire HD falls squarely in the midst of handheld computers generally referred to as tablets, and tablets occupy the market space between smartphones and laptop computers. Tablets generally possess all or nearly all the functions of laptop computers, two notable exceptions being that tablets generally lack physical keyboards and have smaller screens. The appealing feature of tablet computers is that they can run "apps." Apps, short for applications, are small computer programs that run within the tablet's internal memory and literally re-define the operation of the tablet. Apps can give your Kindle Fire HD the ability to act as far more than an e-book reader or a movie player. You can download and install apps that transform your Kindle Fire HD into a digital butler, an electronic medical advisor, a powerful financial analyst, or a first-rate game platform.

Within the tablet marketplace, the Kindle Fire HD is compared favorably to other low-cost ($300 US and under) devices that typically sport 7-inch screens and run apps designed either for the Android operating system or for Apple's iOS operating system. Devices currently in this marketplace include the Apple iPad Mini, Google's Nexus 7, the Samsung Galaxy Tab 3, and the Nook from Barnes and Noble, as well as Amazon's own Kindle Fire HDX.

Where's My Data? (Fire HD Storage & the Amazon Cloud)

With the popularity of tablets, you may have heard talk of what may be a somewhat magical and mystical place known as "the cloud." Your Kindle Fire HD has some built-in data storage, ranging from 8 gigabytes to 64 gigabytes, depending upon the model of Kindle Fire that you purchased.

This may sound like a lot of space, but in the grand scheme of things, it really is not. (By comparison, the average personal computer sold at the time of this writing typically has a 250 gigabyte or 500 gigabyte hard drive, and a single Blu-Ray DVD movie occupies roughly 25 gigabytes.) If you tried to store large amounts of digital content- especially movies and videos- on your Kindle Fire, you would quickly exhaust its usable space. To get around this problem, the Kindle Fire (and many other tablets) store large amounts of information in the cloud, which is another name for data servers that are accessed from the Internet.

Amazon's servers are referred to as the Amazon Cloud, and all Kindle Fire HD owners have access to unlimited amounts of data storage for their purchases in the Amazon cloud.

Content that you purchase from Amazon is stored in either of two places: in your cloud storage on Amazon's servers, and on your Kindle Fire itself. (Often, your content is stored in two places simultaneously: when you download an item, it is stored both on your device, and a copy of it remains in the Amazon cloud.) When you initially purchase a book, a song, a game, or an app (even free content is purchased, you just aren't charged for this), the content is initially stored in your personal space in the Amazon Cloud, where the content is not taking up any space on your Kindle Fire. When you press the Download button that appears on the icon for that content in the cloud, it gets downloaded to the memory space of your Kindle Fire itself.

If you display a given category on your Kindle Fire, such as apps, books, or music, at the top center of the screen you will see icons for *Cloud* and *Device*, as shown in the illustration that follows.

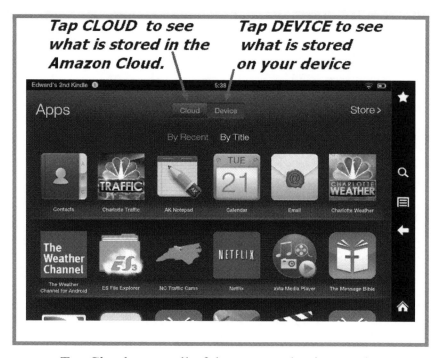

Tap CLOUD to see what is stored in the Amazon Cloud.

Tap DEVICE to see what is stored on your device

Tap Cloud to see all of the content that is stored on Amazon's cloud under your account, and tap Device to see all the content that you downloaded from the cloud onto your device. You can download content from the cloud onto your device anytime you have an active Wi-Fi connection, and you can delete content from the device as necessary to ensure that you have plenty of room for new content. (In the United States, if you have a 3G option on your Kindle Fire, you will not need a Wi-Fi connection, assuming you are within range of a cell phone network. Your Kindle Fire with 3G option will automatically connect to Amazon's network to download from the Amazon cloud when necessary.)

If you are curious as to whether you are running short of storage space on your device, you can quickly determine your available storage space remaining. Get to the Home screen, tap and drag down the Navigation bar at the top of the screen, and tap Settings at the upper right (or tap 'More' on a 1st-gen Fire HD). Under Settings, tap Device at the next screen that appears, then tap Storage. Your Kindle Fire will display a Storage screen, similar to the example shown in the following illustration.

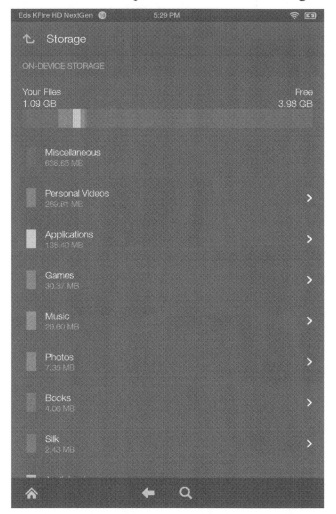

The Storage screen tells you how much space is available, and how much space is currently being used by various categories, such as books and newsstand items, audio books, music, videos, and photos.

History of the Kindle Fire HD

This portion of this chapter certainly isn't required reading if you are to become an accomplished user of your Kindle Fire HD, but it is a fascinating success story. The Kindle Fire HD is one of a line of products that all sprang from the original Amazon Kindle, a revolutionary device inspired by a revolutionary individual, Amazon founder and CEO Jeff Bezos. During the nascent days of the world wide web, it was Bezos who came up with the idea of selling books online, rather than in the traditional bricks and mortar bookstore environment, and Bezos founded Amazon, billed as the world's largest bookstore. Books were very good to Bezos and to Amazon, catapulting the company to a multibillion dollar global enterprise and taking Bezos to billionaire status in the process. But even though Bezos himself was (and is, according to reports) an avid book reader, he recognized something: a cornerstone of Amazon's long-term future in the 21st century, the printed book, was a likely candidate for obsolescence by the end of the 21st century, if not sooner. Music had gone digital, video was in the process of moving in that direction, and for the printed book, the same transition was simply a matter of time. Having built a better bookstore, Bezos believed he could improve upon one of humanity's greatest inventions- the printed book- by taking it digital.

In 2004, Bezos turned a group of engineers loose in an Amazon subsidiary, Lab126, based in Cupertino, California, and charged them with the task of developing a digital replacement for the printed book. Roughly three years later, in November of 2007, Amazon placed the fruits of Bezos dream and the engineers' labors- the original Amazon Kindle- on sale. It used a patented E-ink display that was capable of rendering 16 shades to simulate reading on paper while using minimal amounts of power. Content for the Amazon Kindle could be purchased online and downloaded wirelessly. (The name "Kindle" was the brainchild of consultants hired by the Lab126 division of Amazon, who felt that like kindling, it had the potential to light a fire- and that is exactly what the device began to do in the book publishing world.)

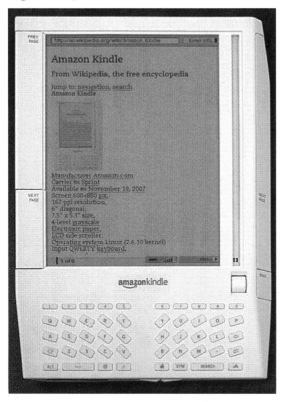

First Amazon Kindle (photo credit: Wikipedia)

Despite the fact that the device cost nearly $400 US, Amazon sold out its initial manufacturing run in a little over five and one half hours, and the Kindle remained out of stock until late April of 2008. The success of the original Amazon Kindle led to a family of devices, and as technology continued to advance and manufacturing costs continued to drop, the Kindle Fire became a product in Amazon's Kindle family. Announced in September of 2011, the original Kindle Fire was Amazon's first Kindle to sport a liquid crystal display-based color screen, rather than the patented black on white E-ink display used by all the earlier Kindles. The Kindle Fire not only included access to Amazon's AppStore, but could also display streaming movies and

TV shows as well as run 'apps,' in addition to being used to read books.

To say that the product has been successful would be an understatement: as of May, 2013, the Kindle Fire HD was the second best-selling tablet after Apple's iPad, with about seven million units sold, according to research estimates (source: Wikipedia). And while there's still a number of years left to this 21st century, the handwriting is clearly on the wall with regards to the eventual demise of the paper-based book. The Association of American Publishers reported that in the first quarter of 2012, e-book sales surpassed those of their paper-based counterparts for the first time- adult eBook sales were reported at $282.3 million, while adult hardcover sales during that same period reached only $229.6 million.

Setting up your Kindle Fire

Set up your Kindle Fire now if it is fresh out of the box. If you've just opened up your Kindle Fire HD's box, you'll need to turn it on and set it up before you can start using it.

If your Kindle Fire is fresh out of the box, you'll need to power up your new tablet and you'll need to set it up before you can begin using it. Before you start, make sure you have your Amazon username and password, and you will also need to be within range of an active Wi-Fi connection (unless you purchased a Fire HD with the 3G option, in which case your device will automatically connect to Amazon's network as long as you are within range of 3G cell phone service).

When you first turn your Kindle Fire on, you'll be asked to choose your language. After doing this, you'll select a Wi-Fi network and enter a password (if yours is a secured network).

The next screen that appears will ask you for registration information. You'll now need to register your Kindle Fire HD.

Enter your Amazon account details, or, if you don't have an Amazon account, choose Create an account and follow the instructions that appear on the screen.

Next, you'll get to choose your time zone, and confirm your account information. Make your selections and tap Continue, and you will be given the option to set up your Facebook and/or Twitter accounts. (You can do this now, or skip this step and save this for later.)

Finally, you will see some on-screen hints and tips that will help you get started with your Kindle Fire HD. If you already have Kindle content linked to your device, or apps from the Amazon App Store, they will all be available for download from the Amazon Cloud (more on this topic shortly). Your recently-read Kindle books will appear in an area known as the carousel automatically, along with the latest apps and other downloaded content.

Controls and Layout, 2nd-Generation Kindle Fire HD

Take the time to get familiar with the physical aspects of your Kindle Fire. Looking at the rear of the device, with the Amazon logo facing right-side upwards, the following illustration shows the layout of various components.

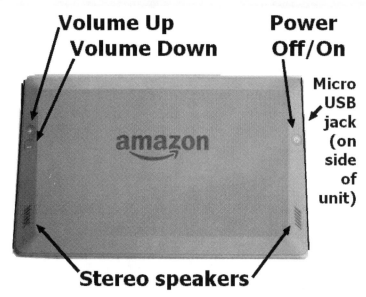

Volume Up
Volume Down

Power Off/On

Micro USB jack (on side of unit)

Stereo speakers

Kindle Fire HD component layout (2013 model)

A major improvement of the second-gen Fire HD involved a simple re-positioning of the volume up/down and power buttons to a beveled edge on the rear. (Thank you, Amazon engineering, because the buttons on the first-gen Fire HD were a real pain to reach at times!)

Controls and Layout, 1st-Generation Kindle Fire HD

If you happen to own a first-generation Kindle Fire, you should become familiar with the physical layout of your tablet. With the device held with its built-in camera (the small circle) at the top of the screen, the right edge contains the off/on switch, a rocker-style volume control, and a headphone jack, as shown in this illustration.

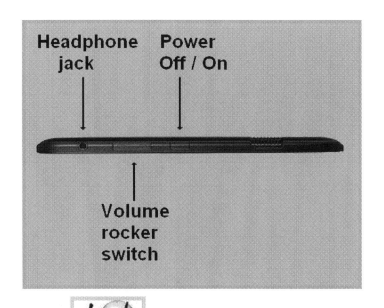

Get familiar with the various parts of the Kindle Fire's user interface. The next chapter will detail this area extensively, but out of the box, it helps to know about the areas that you will be working with on your Kindle Fire HD screen. The following illustration shows these areas.

(Second-gen Fire HD)

If you happen to own a first-gen Fire HD, there are minor differences in the display, but it takes on a similar appearance, as shown in the following illustration.

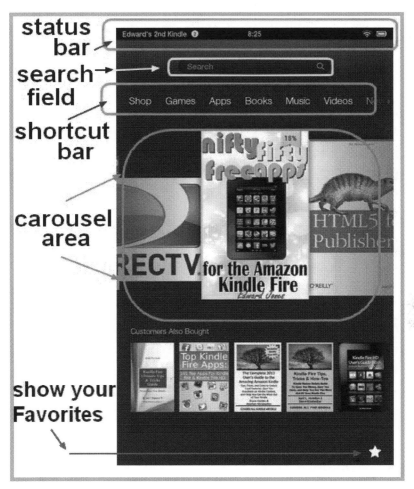

status bar
search field
shortcut bar
carousel area
show your Favorites

(First-gen Fire HD)

You can get quick access to items that you use regularly by placing them in your Favorites area. (You can view all of your favorites by swiping the entire screen upwards with one finger on the second-gen Fire HD, or you can tap the star icon at the bottom right of the screen on a first-gen Fire HD.) To add a book, periodical, or app to your favorites area, first use the Navigation bar at the top of the screen. When the desired category appears, press and hold a desired item until a popup menu appears, then select Add to Home from the menu.

To install any saved apps, in the Navigation Bar tap on Apps, then tap on the Cloud tab. Tap on any of the icons to start that particular app downloading onto your device.

You can import your iTunes or similar music collection from your computer to your Kindle Fire. To import an existing music collection, you'll have to set up the Amazon Cloud Player on your tablet. Open a browser window on your computer, and visit amazon.com/cloudplayer (if you are in North America) or visit amazon.co.uk/cloudplayer (if you are in the United Kingdom) to begin importing the music from your computer into Cloud Player, which can then be streamed or downloaded onto your Kindle Fire HD.

Having problems??? When in doubt, reboot. Your Kindle Fire HD is a sophisticated computer, and like all computers, it may hiccup for unexplainable reasons at times. If your Fire HD freezes or locks up and refuses to respond to any actions, perform a hard reset. (You needn't worry about losing any memory settings with this type of reset; it just halts any programs currently running and shuts down your device.) Hold the power button depressed for at least 20 seconds and then release the button. Wait another 10 seconds, then turn on your Kindle Fire.

If you are experiencing an unusually high number of system lock-ups, make sure your battery charge level is not very low. A nearly fully-drained battery is a common cause of random Kindle Fire freezes.

Chapter 2: User-Interface Tips, Tricks, and Traps

The *user interface* (that's techno-speak for "the way you get along with the device") is fairly intuitive on a Kindle Fire, and that is by design. Amazon engineers have done a credible job of making the tablet easy to use, and with a market dominated by a product like Apple's iPad, that was an understandable goal. Nevertheless, there are things that you can do to make the way that you use your Kindle Fire more efficient, and that is what this chapter is all about.

About the Home Screen, Navigation Bar, Carousel, and Favorites

The Kindle Fire HD is based on a heavily modified version of Google's Android operating system. For the technically minded among readers, the first generation Fire HD was based on the Honeycomb version of the Android operating system, and upgrades to later models in existence resulted in the last shipments of first-gen units based on the Ice Cream Sandwich version of the Android operating system. The second generation Fire HD utilizes a heavily customized version of the Android operating system. Based on the Jelly Bean release of the Android O/S, the current Fire HD and all models in the Kindle Fire line (including both Kindle Fire HDX models) use a version of the Android operating system that Google developed exclusively for Amazon, known as Fire 3.0 O/S.

In any case, all Kindle Fires make use of a user interface that is very different than that of a generic Android tablet. Power up a Kindle Fire and you won't see the desktop like design of an Android tablet. Instead, you will see Amazon's own customized interface called the Home screen, shown in the next illustration. Pardon the intentional repetition, but the illustration, which was shown in the prior chapter, is displayed once more here. In this chapter, we go into more detail about the parts of the Kindle Fire user interface, and how you can best use these features.

(The Home screen of the second-gen Kindle Fire HD)

From the Home screen, your books, apps, music, and videos are all accessible with a swipe of the ***Navigation Bar***. Simply swipe the Navigation bar to the left or right and tap the desired category such as apps, games, books, music, or videos to display all of the items within that category. And there is a ***Search icon*** (in the shape of a magnifying glass) that can be used to search the entire device content, to search Amazon's massive library of content, or to just search the web.

The center area of the Home screen displays the ***Carousel***. The Carousel will contain an assortment of icons for

28

all of the items that you've recently accessed on your Kindle Fire, whether they are books, songs, magazines, movies, or web pages.

Understand the difference between the Carousel and your *Favorites*. The Carousel grows dynamically as you use your Kindle Fire, because an icon for everything that you've recently used on your Kindle Fire will appear on the Carousel and will remain for some time unless you delete it from the Carousel. With your Favorites, on the other hand, nothing appears automatically. You must add an item to the Favorites area in order for it to appear. (On a new Kindle Fire, it's true that a few items appear in the Favorites area, but Amazon added these items so that the Favorites would not be empty. Clearly, these are not your favorites, so you'll probably want to get rid of them.)

You can get quick access to items that you use regularly by placing them in your Favorites. You can view all of your favorites by swiping the entire screen upwards with one finger on the second-gen Fire HD, or you can tap the star icon at the bottom right of the screen on a first-gen Fire HD. To add a book, song, movie, game, or app to your favorites area, first use the Navigation bar at the top of the screen. When the desired category appears, press and hold a desired item until a popup menu appears, then select Add to Home from the menu.

Clean up your Carousel. Over time, your Carousel can become overly cluttered with icons for all the items you've accessed on your Kindle Fire. To delete items from the carousel, press and hold the unwanted item until a popup menu appears, and select Remove from Carousel from the menu.

Know how to come home. One of the first things any young child learns is how to come home, and any new Kindle Fire user should know how to get to the home screen as well. From anywhere you are at, tap in the center of the screen, and the home icon will appear at the lower left. Tap Home and you will return to the home screen.

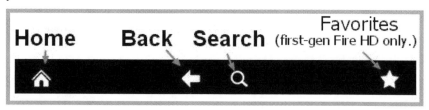

Setting your Display

Adjust your font sizes to make reading easiest on YOU. The Kindle Fire HD is a great multimedia device, but the entire Kindle line began life as an e-book reader, and millions of people still use it primarily for that purpose. You can easily adjust the font sizes to fit your needs. With any book open, tap in the center of the screen, and then tap View (Aa). You will see a dialog box like the one shown in the following illustration:

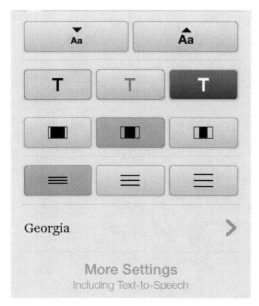

Tap the small letters 'Aa' to shrink the text, or tap the large letters 'Aa' to enlarge the text. You can also try the different Color Mode settings (white, sepia, and black) to see if you prefer one of these different backgrounds for your book reading. The lower rows within the dialog box contain buttons that let you adjust the margin width or the line spacing. And you can tap the Font name list box (displaying 'Georgia' in this illustration) to display additional fonts that you can choose for your display.

Tap the 'More Settings' link at the bottom of the dialog box, and another screen appears where you can choose to turn on Popular Highlights and Text-to-Speech options. These options, enabled by the publishers of some books and periodicals, allow for the display of highlighted items that other readers find to be popular, and allow for the reading of text aloud, using the built-in speakers or the headphone jack of your Kindle Fire.

The process is slightly different with a first generation Fire HD. Open any book, tap in the center of a page, then tap Settings at the upper left. When the Settings dialog box appears as shown below, tap the small letters 'Aa' to shrink the text, or tap the large letters 'Aa' to enlarge the text. You can also try the

31

different Color Mode settings (white, sepia, and black) to see if you prefer one of these different backgrounds for your book reading.

Note that the Kindle display settings will control the text display of most e-books, but may not have an effect on some magazines. Many of the magazine publishers use their own settings menus to change the way the magazine is displayed.

Customizing your Favorites

Edit and rearrange your Favorites. Any items that you recently accessed will appear on the Carousel. You can add any of these items to your Favorites so that you can gain fast access to regularly used items by swiping the entire screen upwards (2nd gen Fire HD) or by pressing the "star" button (1st-gen. Fire HD). Just find the item in your Carousel, press and hold, then press 'Add to Home' from the menu options that appear in the popup menu.

You can rearrange the items in your Favorites area to suit your liking. Just long-press on an item, then slide your finger to a new location. The remaining favorites will automatically rearrange themselves.

Use 'Search' to find anything stored on your Kindle. While many Kindle Fire users think of the search field as a way to search for content such as books or movies, you can actually use the Search field to find any item that is stored on your device. Just go to the Home screen, tap the magnifying glass to bring up the Search field, and type a few letters. Search will bring up all items- books, videos, music, games, and so on- that match the letters you've typed. Tap anywhere above the keyboard to put the keyboard away, scroll to the desired item, and tap the item to open the item or launch an app.

Changing Basic Settings on your Kindle Fire

Know your status. At the top of your Kindle Fire, just above the Navigation bar, is an area known as the Status bar. Here, you will see any notifications indicated by a number inside a small circle, a wi-fi signal strength indicator, and the battery life indicator. Tap and drag down anywhere within the Status bar or Navigation bar areas to reveal various settings for your Kindle Fire, as shown in the following illustration:

Auto-rotate: your Kindle Fire contains a gyroscope, which senses when the device is rotated, causing the display to shift between portrait and landscape mode. There are times when this is more of an annoyance than a help, such as when you are reading with the Kindle lying on a flat surface such as a tabletop. Tap the Auto-rotate icon to change the setting to locked, to disable the auto rotate function. (On a first generation Kindle Fire HD, this option is labeled 'Locked' or 'Unlocked.')

Brightness: tap the brightness icon to reveal a slider bar that you can slide up or down to increase or decrease screen brightness.

Wireless: Tapping the wireless option brings up another screen which lets you enable or disable Airplane Mode (turning off wireless transmission for when you are using your Kindle Fire in flight), along with an option to enable Bluetooth device settings (for sharing data with other Bluetooth-equipped devices such as many modern laptops, portable keyboards, and some smart phones). You will also find an option to allow or prevent Location Based Services from estimating your location. Also present on this screen is a Wi-Fi option that, when tapped, displays all wireless networks that are broadcasting in your area, similar to the example shown in the following illustration.

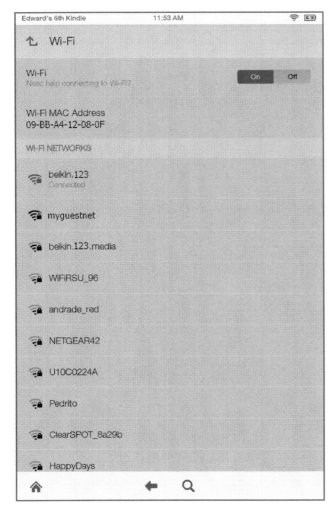

Edward's 6th Kindle   11:53 AM

⤴ Wi-Fi

Wi-Fi
Need help connecting to Wi-Fi?
     On   Off

Wi-Fi MAC Address
09-BB-A4-12-08-0F

WI-FI NETWORKS

belkin.123
Connected

myguestnet

belkin.123.media

WiFiRSU_96

andrade_red

NETGEAR42

U10C0224A

Pedrito

ClearSPOT_8a29b

HappyDays

   ⌂   ←   Q

     On this screen, select the desired Wi-Fi network by name. If the network is protected, you will be asked for the security key, and you must enter the security key before your Kindle Fire will connect to your Wi-Fi network.

If you don't remember what the security key is for your own home Wi-Fi network, look on the bottom of the cable modem or the phone company router that provides your Wi-Fi service. Many Wi-Fi routers provided by cable and telephone companies have the password written on a sticker on the underside of the modem.

Quiet Time: This option lets you turn on "quiet time," disabling any popup notifications and muting all sounds for message notifications such as e-mail or calendar alerts.

Help: This icon, when pressed, displays a help screen that lets you get help with wireless connectivity issues, open the user guide for your Kindle Fire HD, or contact Amazon customer service, either via e-mail or by phone.

Settings: Tapping the settings icon will display a settings screen, as shown in the example that follows.

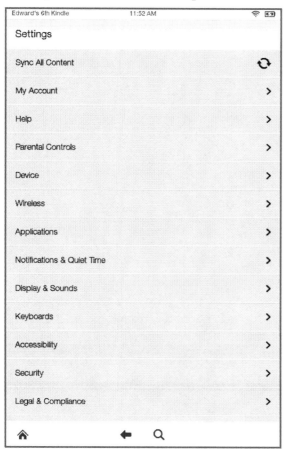

From here, you can access a variety of settings for your Kindle Fire HD, by simply tapping on the appropriate subcategory within the Settings screen. For example, you can tap the Display and Sounds subcategory to display a screen that lets you adjust the volume and or the screen brightness, and you can tap the Security subcategory to create a locking password that prevents your Kindle Fire from being used by unauthorized users who do not know the password that you set for your device. You'll find many of these individual subcategories and their options explained in further detail in later parts of this book.

Of particular interest is the Device subcategory under the Settings screen. (To get here, drag down the Notifications bar at the top of the screen, and tap the Settings icon at the upper-right. In the Settings screen, tap Device to reveal the screen shown in the following illustration.) Here you can gain access to a number of settings that govern the individual behavior of your Kindle Fire HD.

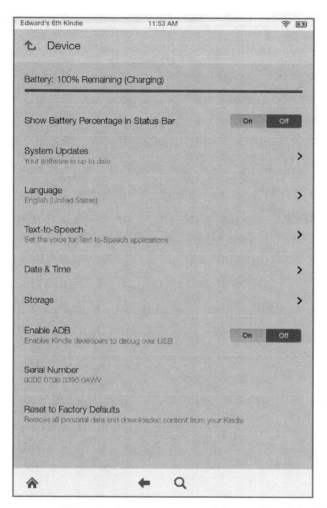

The Device screen provides a visual indication of the state of your battery charge, the language used by your device when it displays or prompts for information, and the storage space utilized by various applications such as books, magazines, movies, music, and so forth. You can select a desired voice used with the Text-to-Speech feature (or download additional voices), adjust your date and time settings, and even reset the device to its original factory settings (useful when it is time to upgrade to a more powerful Fire HDX, and pass on your trusted Fire HD to a close friend or relative).

Sync: (1ST-gen. Kindle Fire HD only) -tapping the Sync icon will synchronize the content of your Kindle Fire with the Amazon Cloud, and your email, contacts, and calendar will be synchronized with external sources, assuming you have set up these external sources. (On a 2nd gen Fire HD, you can synchronize your device by tapping the Settings icon, then tapping 'Sync All Content.' Also, note that you can find out how to setup the external sources such as your e-mail, contacts, and calendar in Chapter 6, Email Tips, Tricks and Traps.)

Volume: (1ST-gen. Kindle Fire HD only) -tapping the volume icon displays a slider bar on the screen, and you can finger swipe the slider bar left or right to increase or decrease the volume. (On a second generation Fire HD, it's easier to adjust the volume simply by pressing the buttons on the rear of the device.)

General Typing and Text-Entry Tips

Make the keyboard larger. Most Kindle Fire apps work in portrait or landscape mode, and the keyboard is much larger and easier to use in landscape mode. Rotate the Kindle Fire 90 degrees to get a landscape view of the keyboard, for an easier typing experience.

When typing large amounts of text, end each sentence with a fast double-space. Heavy duty word processing on a Kindle Fire (or any similarly sized tablet) is going to be somewhat challenging due to the combination of a soft keyboard and small screen size. One time saving tip when doing a lot of typing on the Kindle Fire is at the end of each sentence, tap the spacebar quickly twice. A fast double-space will automatically insert a period, followed by a single space. You can then continue on to the next sentence.

The Kindle Fire really does have a Caps Lock key. For those times when you need to type a string of characters as ALL UPPERCASE LETTERS, the Kindle Fire does have the equivalent of a PC's Caps Lock key. Just double-tap the Shift key, and an orange bar will appear underneath the Shift symbol on the key indicator indicating that you are in Caps Lock mode. Type your upper case letters, then press the Shift key once more to drop out of Caps Lock mode.

Use the numbers shortcut to quickly enter numbers. If you are typing text, you don't need to switch between the letters keyboard and the numbers and symbols keyboard just to enter a number. The top row of letters can be long-pressed to enter a number. From left to right, a long-press on any of the top row of keys produce numbers from 1 through 9, followed by 0. Press and hold a top row letter until a number appears in orange, then release, to type that number.

Use the second and third row keyboard keys for most commonly used punctuation characters. If you closely examine the Kindle Fire HD's soft keyboard, you will see various non-alpha characters displayed at the upper right corner of each key. If you perform a long press on a particular key, the character shown in the upper-right corner of the key will appear, and you can release your finger to enter that character.

Your finger can serve as an insertion pointer. When editing large amounts of text, tap your finger on any empty area to display the Editing Tool. You can then press on it and move your fingertip within the text that you already typed, then release and edit the text as desired. When done editing, tap again at the end of the text, and continue typing.

Access the Cut-Copy-and-Paste options with a long-press on any word. If you need to cut or copy and paste during text editing, long-press on any single word, and cut / copy / paste editing options will appear, along with two selection handles. Drag the selection handles to highlight the desired text, then long-press on the desired text, and choose Cut or Copy. To paste the cut or copied text elsewhere, just long press at the desired location, and tap Paste.

Chapter 3: Free Books, Movies, and Music Tips, Tricks and Traps

Your Kindle Fire HD is a great source of reading and entertainment, but let's face it: content costs, and quality contents costs more. Like everyone else, authors and songwriters certainly expect to eat (no surprise there), and production costs skyrocket when you get into the league of big-name entertainers and the costs of producing those Hollywood blockbusters that you're fond of watching on the 'small screen'. But there are great sources of free, quality content available for your Kindle Fire. My favorite source is one that in a way, you've likely already paid for (and continue paying for) over the years: I'm speaking of your tax-supported, local public library.

Getting Kindle Books from your local library

Borrow Kindle content for free from your public library. Many Kindle owners are oblivious to the fact that most public libraries now loan books, movies, music, and other digital content for the Amazon Kindle line of e-readers (as well as for other digital products like smartphones, Apple iPads, and other tablet computers.) In the United States alone, at the time of this writing, nearly 20,000 public libraries are members of a system called OverDrive Media. OverDrive Media provides an app for your Kindle Fire HD that lets you borrow content electronically from your public library. All you'll need is the app (a free download from the Amazon store) and your library card number. Check with your local library to see if they are a member of the OverDrive program. You should be able to check without getting out of your easy chair; do a Google search for your town's public library web site, and once you find it, look for a link that says "download e-books" or something similar. If your city does not have a membership in such a program, there are libraries that allow nonresidents to obtain a library card for an annual fee. Two, at the time of this writing, are those of Fairfax County, Virginia (www.fairfaxcounty.gov/library for more information) and the City of Philadelphia (www.freelibrary.org for more information).

Once you've found that your library is a member of the OverDrive Media service, go to the Amazon App store, search on the term 'overdrive', and download the app to your Kindle Fire HD. Launch the app, and you'll be asked for a ZIP code; enter your zip code, and you'll see your local library's name in a list. Select your library by name, and you'll be taken to a page for your local library, where you can borrow books, movies, and other digital content. Browse among what your library has available for lending, click on a title, and you'll be taken to an Amazon page with the book, but in place of the "Buy with one click" button, you'll see a "Borrow from library" button. Click that button, and the book will be downloaded to your Kindle Fire.

Different libraries have different lending policies, so you'll want to check with your local library to determine the exact length of your loan. In my resident town of Charlotte, North Carolina, books have a two-week loan with one possible renewal, and movies are good for ten days. Many libraries now offer regularly scheduled classes or workshops that teach library patrons how to download digital content, so you may want to visit your local library and sign up for such a class in your home town.

Using the Kindle Owner's Lending Library ("KOLL") to your advantage

The second great free source of books is Amazon's own Kindle Owners Lending Library. If you are a member of Amazon Prime, you owe it to yourself to check out the Kindle Owners' Lending Library. The Kindle Owners Lending Library allows Amazon Prime members to borrow one book at a time each month, at no cost. There are thousands of books available through the service, and you can find free books to borrow through the Kindle Owners Lending Library using these steps:

1. At the Kindle Fire store, click "See all categories." When the list of various categories (Books, Kindle Singles, Kindle Newsstand, New & Noteworthy, etc.) appears, click the Kindle Owners' Lending Library option.

2. After picking the Kindle Owners' Lending Library, you can browse a list of books to borrow. You will know that a book is eligible for borrowing because it will have a "Prime" badge attached.

3. Click the 'Borrow' tab. Next, you'll see a "Buy for $xx.xx" tab and a "Borrow for Free" tab. Click the "Borrow for Free" tab, and your borrowed book will be downloaded to your Kindle Fire.

Easily Search the Kindle Store on your Fire for Free Books

A third great way to find free books is to search for... free books! As part of regular ongoing promotions, many authors will place their books on sale for nothing during certain days of a 90-day period, as part of an authors' program called Amazon KDP Select. You can take advantage of this fact by simply searching among any desired genre of Kindle books, and entering "0.00" as your search criteria in the Search box. What appears will be every Kindle book that has a price of zero dollars, zero cents on that particular day. (And before you think that checking this list would result in a limited selection, you should know that on any given day there are hundreds of free books offered through Amazon's promotional program.) This list of books will change wildly on a daily basis, so if you're an avid reader, you may find it worth your while to perform this sort of a search on a regular basis.

Download free books from the Internet, and transfer these to your Kindle Fire HD using your USB cable. The final source of free books that this chapter will detail is that of the Internet itself. You can find countless sources of free e-books on the Internet. These come in a variety of file formats; besides its own native file format of Kindle (.azw) files, your Kindle Fire HD will also read books in Adobe Acrobat (.PDF) format, in MobiPocket (.MOBI) format, or in plain text (.TXT) format. Unfortunately, your Kindle Fire HD will NOT read files in the popular E-PUB format used by the Sony e-reader, the Barnes and Noble NOOK, and many other e-readers. The solution for this is not overwhelmingly complex; you can download free e-book converter programs that will convert e-books from most other formats into Amazon's Kindle (.KZW) format. An excellent program is called Calibre (go to www.calibre-ebook.com for details). Calibre can convert files from many formats, including the E-PUB format, into the Amazon Kindle file format. Once you convert the file, use the file transfer techniques described in Chapter 5 of this book, to transfer the e-books that you've converted to your Kindle Fire HD.

As for sources, performing a Google search for "free e-books" will return an avalanche of sites. Here is a small list to get you started:

Project Gutenberg- www.gutenberg.org

ManyBooks.net- http://manybooks.net

Google Books- http://books.google.com/

MobiPocket Free Books-www.mobipocket.com/freebooks/

An exhaustive source of free computer-based books can be found at http://freecomputerbooks.com. Finally, you'll find a surprisingly comprehensive list of textbooks that can be legally shared, at http://textbookrevolution.org. These are in .PDF format.

Chapter 4: Silk browser tips, tricks, and traps

The Amazon Silk web browser for the Kindle Fire is unique among web browsers, engineered from the ground up especially for the Kindle Fire. Since Android-based tablets will certainly run established browsers such as Google Chrome and Mozilla Firefox, many have wondered why Amazon chose to design a new browser from scratch. The answer is, Amazon wanted to offer a fast browsing experience, so the browser design splits tasks between the browser software that is running locally on the Kindle Fire, and Amazon's Cloud Servers. As a result of this unique design, a number of features are familiar to you because you've seen them in other browsers, but there are a few that are unique to the Silk browser.

Surfing the Web with the Silk Browser

To launch the Silk browser, at the Home screen, finger-swipe the Navigation bar near the top to the far right and tap Web. The illustration on the following page shows the various parts of the Silk browser.

The Silk browser is a tabbed browser, like Google's Chrome, Mozilla Firefox, and more recent versions of Microsoft Internet Explorer. To open a new tab, just tap the plus sign in the top right corner. You can then tap in the Search field of the new tab, and enter the desired web address.

If you are viewing a page and there is a link embedded in the page and you would like to go to that link in a separate tab, give the link a long press rather than a tap. A menu of options will appear, and you can choose 'Open in new tab' from the menu.

Share web pages with your friends. When a page is displayed in the Silk browser, the Quick menu button at the bottom of the browser window will include a Share Page symbol. Tap this symbol, and you can send a link to the page either via email, or through Facebook or Twitter.

The "thumb and finger spread" or "thumb and finger pinch" works in the Silk browser. You will often encounter web pages with text that is too small to read on the Kindle Fire screen. Place your thumb and finger on the screen and spread them to magnify, or pinch them together to reduce the magnification.

Use "Find on this page" as a search tool. Oftentimes you will need to search a website for a particular word or phrase. To do this in the Silk browser, tap the menu button at the bottom of the window, then tap "Find in page." Enter a search term in the search field that appears, and use the up and down arrow keys to move through the search results.

Let the browser complete your entry. As you begin typing characters into the search / address field, a list of suggestions appears below the field. Type more characters, and suggestions increase in accuracy. When you see a suggestion that matches the URL you intended to type, tap that suggestion.

Using Bookmarks

Bookmark commonly visited pages so you can return to them quickly at a later time. As with all modern web browsers, the Silk browser provides the ability to bookmark sites so that you can easily return to the same site. To add a bookmark, tap the Quick Menu icon at the bottom of the browser window then tap Add Bookmark. (On a 1st-gen Fire HD, tap the page tab itself, then tap the plus symbol to the left of the URL). With any build of Fire HD, you will now see the Add Bookmarks dialog box. Change the name of the entry to something friendlier if you desire, and tap OK, to add the page to your bookmarked pages.

Quickly get to your bookmarked pages. There are different ways to go to a bookmarked page, but this method seems to involve the least amount of steps. Tap the Menu icon at the top left and drag the Silk sidebar out. Tap Bookmarks, locate the desired bookmark, perform a long press on the icon, and choose Open in New Tab from the menu that appears to open that webpage.

Delete any bookmark page that's no longer needed. From the Bookmarks page (get there by tapping the Menu icon at the top left, dragging the Silk sidebar out, and tapping Bookmarks), perform a long-press on the unwanted bookmark, and choose "Delete Bookmark" from the menu that appears. (On a 1st-gen Fire HD, you can go to the bookmarked page, press the plus icon to the left of the URL, and tap "Delete Bookmark" in the dialog box that appears.)

Changing Silk Settings for Best Operation

Choose your preferred search engine. The default search engine for the Silk browser is Google, but if you prefer to use Microsoft Bing or Yahoo as your default search engine, you can change the Silk browser to either of these options. Pull down the Navigation bar, tap Settings (or tap 'More' on a 1st-gen Fire HD), go to Applications > Silk Browser > Search Engine, and make your desired choice.

Keep Silk performance up through regular housecleaning. Just as browsers on your PC can be slowed over time from too many cookies or from a clogged cache, so can the Silk browser. You can perform a bit of browser housecleaning on occasion by dragging down the Navigation bar, going to Settings > Applications > Silk Browser, and tapping the Clear History, Clear Cache, and Clear All Cookies data options.

Set your Silk settings to your preferences. The Silk browser has a number of settings that you can use to change the operation of the browser. Pull down the Navigation bar, tap Settings (or tap 'More' on a 1st-gen Fire HD), and go to Applications > Silk Browser. You will see the settings that apply to the browser, as shown in the following illustration.

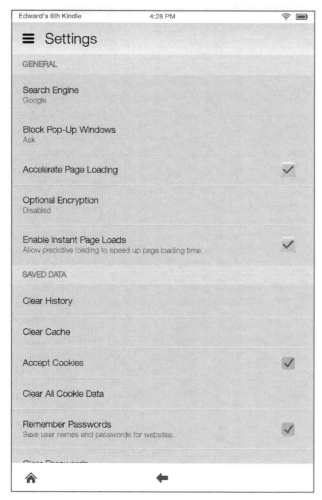

(Silk browser settings, 2nd-generation Fire HD)

If you happen to own a 1st-gen Fire HD, you will find that the options have minor differences, but generally cover the same areas. The Silk browser options for the 1st-gen Fire HD are sho0wn in the illustration that follows.

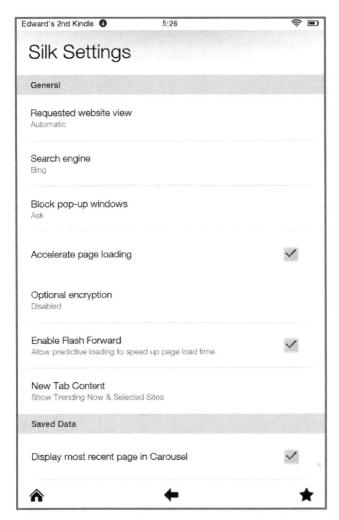

(Silk browser settings, 1ˢᵗ-generation Fire HD)

These settings affect the way the Silk Browser behaves in various ways. Requested Website View is normally set to automatic, but you can change this to desktop or mobile. Under Search Engine, you can specify the desired search engine used by the browser, and you can choose to block popup windows. The Accelerate Page Loading and Enable Instant Page Loads options are by default set to on; however you may wish to consider turning off Accelerate Page Loading; see the tip 'Speed Up the

Performance of The Silk Browser' later in this chapter for further details about this topic.

If you scroll down in the Silk Settings screen, you will see additional options revealed. These include whether or not you want to display the most recent page visited within the carousel, and whether you want to clear the history, the cache, and accept cookies or clear cookie data from the browser. You also have options to remember passwords used when visiting sites, to clear all passwords from the browser memory, and whether or not to remember form data or to clear form data. You can enable location tracking or clear location access, and under Advanced Settings, you can choose whether images are normally loaded, whether JavaScript is enabled, and whether security warnings are enabled.

Speed up the performance of the Silk browser. At the time the original Kindle Fire was introduced, much hoopla was made as to the split nature of the browser design, part browser in the device and part browser in the Amazon Cloud, and the promise of speed offered by this unique design. In practice, the hype hasn't exactly met reality, as one of the biggest complaints about the Silk browser has been its slow speed in processing most web pages.

The problem is, there is hype, and then there is the real world. In the real world, the Silk browser in its default settings is trying to be a desktop browser within a small 7 inch screen. As a result, the browser is trying to zoom in on every single page load, something that is simply not necessary in an overwhelming majority of cases. You are likely to see a faster response from the Silk browser if you change the following setting (drag down the Navigation bar and go to Settings > Applications > Silk Browser)

Accelerate Page Loading: turn this OFF

Once you make this change, you are likely to see an increase in speed with the majority of web pages that you visit using the Silk browser. (If your experience differs, you can always change this settings back to its original value.)

Chapter 5: File Management Tips, Tricks, and Traps

In press reviews, the Kindle Fire has taken a fair share of criticism for being a relatively "closed ecosystem," according to its critics. Many reviewers have claimed that Kindle Fire owners are dependent on purchasing virtually all content from Amazon. In the opinion of this author, that reputation is somewhat undeserved. Certainly, it is in Amazon's interest to get you to buy your content from Amazon. But the 'closed ecosystem' claim made by many members of the press implies that you must purchase all your content from Amazon, and that is simply not the case. In addition to purchasing content from the Amazon store, you can find millions (literally!) of books from other sources, and these can be copied to your Kindle Fire from your computer using the USB cable that is a part of your charging assembly. The Kindle Fire uses the .mobi file format for its e-books, and e-books in the .mobi format can be found in thousands of places all over the internet, some paid, and others free. There are also millions of books in the popular E-PUB format used by Sony and by Google, and there are free converters readily available from hundreds of sources on the web that will convert files from the E-PUB format into the .mobi format used by all Amazon Kindles.

You can use the same USB cable techniques to copy MP3, AAC, or WAV files that you obtain from your own sources, and these become a part of the music library on your Kindle Fire. There are apps like Crackle that let you stream any one of thousands of free movies or TV shows to your Kindle Fire. If you are already a Netflix subscriber, you can download the Netflix app from the Amazon app store (the app is free) and watch any content that you would normally obtain from Netflix on your Kindle Fire. And short length, personal movies compatible with the Kindle Fire (in 3gp or mp4 format) can also be copied to the device, although the 8 gigabyte memory size is by nature going to limit the length of movies that can be stored locally on the device. (By comparison, an average Blu-ray DVD occupies 25 gigabytes of disk space.)

You can also email documents directly to your Kindle Fire, using Amazon's free Send to Kindle service. Every registered Kindle has its own assigned email address, and you can send certain types of files- Microsoft Word documents, rich text (RTF) or text (TXT) files, .JPG or .PNG graphics files, Adobe PDF files, and others- to your Kindle Fire's assigned email address. (See the following heading if you do not know your Kindle Fire's assigned e-mail address.) Within roughly 5 minutes of the time that you send a file as an attachment, it will show up on your Kindle Fire, in the Documents folder. You can then tap the document to open it and read it in the native Kindle Viewer, and there are apps available that will let you edit Microsoft Word documents on your Kindle.

To take full advantage of all of these features of the Kindle Fire, you'll need to know how to use the file management features of the Kindle Fire. You'll find the various tips, tricks, and traps that pertain to these topics covered throughout this chapter.

Sending Files to your Kindle Fire via E-mail

Know your Fire's email address. If you purchased your Kindle Fire directly from Amazon, it was registered for you when it arrived. If you purchased it from a retailer such as Best Buy, you may have gone through the setup steps on your own. In either case, your Kindle Fire has been assigned a Send to Kindle email address. This address is something similar to *username@kindle.com*. To see your email address, pull down the Navigation bar, tap Settings (or tap 'More' on a 1st-gen Fire HD), and under Settings, tap My Account. You will see a message that reads something like-

Edward's second Kindle is registered to Edward Jones
edjones45@kindle.com

This is the email address that you can use to send files as attachments to your Kindle Fire.

Before you can send any documents to your Kindle Fire, you must add the sending email address to an "Approved personal document email list" under your Amazon account settings. To prevent Kindle owners from receiving unwanted spam, Amazon blocks any email sent to a Kindle address at Kindle.com that hasn't been added to the approved personal document email list. Log into your Amazon account in a computer's web browser, and under the 'Your Account' link, click 'Manage Your Kindle.' At the next screen that appears, you'll see all your Kindle devices (assuming you own more than one). If you own just one Kindle Fire HD, you will see just that device. Scroll down and locate the desired Kindle in your list of devices, click the Edit link to the right of the device name, and you will be able to change the e-mail address registered to that Kindle. You can also add authorized e-mail addresses that will be permitted to send e-mail to your Kindle. By default, Amazon adds the e-mail address that is associated with your Amazon account. To add authorized addresses, under 'Your Kindle Account' at the left, click Personal Document Settings, then look for the Approved Personal Document E-mail List near the bottom of the screen. You can click the 'Add a new Approved E-mail Address' link in this area to add another email address.

Once you've added your email address to the approved personal document email list, you can attach files to an email message and send it to your send to kindle address. Documents can be in the form of .DOC, .DOCX, .RTF, .TXT, .HTM or .HTML, ZIP, .MOBI, and .AZW file formats. Images can be sent in the .JPG, .PNG, .GIF, or .BMP file formats. The conversion process assumes an active wi-fi (or 3G) connection, since Amazon's Send to Kindle service converts your file into Amazon's own .AZW file format, then downloads it to your Kindle Fire using Amazon's Whispernet.

Attachments cannot be larger than 50 megabytes per attachment, and each email must not have more than 25 attachments. If any of your files are larger than 50 megabytes, the Send to Kindle process will fail for that file, and that file will not appear in your Documents folder.

3G model owners, use a Wi-Fi network where possible to avoid extra charges from the the Send to Kindle service. If you own a Kindle Fire HD with the 3G option, be aware that Amazon adds a small surcharge to your account for each use of their 3G network when used by the Send to Kindle service. You can avoid these surcharges if you use a Wi-Fi network rather than Amazon's 3G service to receive files that you send to your Kindle.

Use the Send to Kindle service to convert PDF files to Amazon readable documents. In addition to the file types listed in the previous tip, you can also send PDF files to your Kindle, and Amazon uses a conversion service to convert the PDF file into Amazon's own .AZW file format. Simply add the word "convert" to the subject line of your email, then attach the PDF file and send the email to your Send to Kindle email address.

Moving Files to your Fire HD with your USB Cable

You can also transfer files from a laptop or desktop computer to your Kindle Fire, using a USB to micro-USB cable. This is the same cable that is supplied as a charging cable for your Kindle Fire; one end contains the micro USB connector that plugs into the base of your Kindle Fire, and the other end contains a standard USB connector. Use the cable to connect your Kindle Fire to your computer, and the Fire will appear as a USB flash drive under your computer's operating system.

Users of Windows XP may have to install additional software before using a USB cable to access the Kindle Fire, and the users of the Apple Mac will have to install additional software. Go to the following link for additional details:

http://www.kindle.com/support/downloads

Once the Kindle Fire appears as a USB drive under your computer's operating system, you can simply drag and drop or copy and paste the desired files into the appropriate folders of the Kindle Fire.

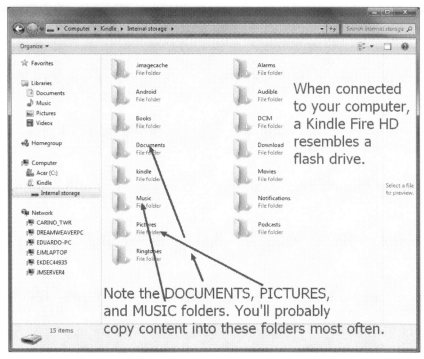

When connected to your computer, a Kindle Fire HD resembles a flash drive.

Note the DOCUMENTS, PICTURES, and MUSIC folders. You'll probably copy content into these folders most often.

You can use a USB cable to transfer files in the form of .DOC, .DOCX, .XLS, .PPT, .RTF, .TXT, .HTM or .HTML, ZIP, .MOBI' and .AZW file formats. Images can be in the .JPG, .PNG, .GIF, or .BMP file formats, and audio files can be in the .AAC, .MP3, .MIDI, .OGG, or .WAV file formats.

The built in file viewer that is included with your Kindle Fire will allow you to open and view files in the common Microsoft office formats, but you will not be able to edit these files. If you wish to edit these files, there are apps available from the Amazon app store that will let you edit Microsoft Office files. The author happens to like QuickOffice Pro, which is priced at a cost of just under $10.00 at the time of this writing, and there are other similar apps, including Kingsoft Office by Kingsoft, and Documents to Go by DataWiz.

Move Files Wirelessly with the Wi-Fi File Explorer App

You can transfer files to your Kindle Fire HD wirelessly ('look ma, no cables!') Assuming you have a home network with PCs attached to it, you don't necessarily have to resort to the annoyance of a cable connected between your Kindle Fire and your computer every time you want to move a file between the two. Wi-Fi File Explorer is a neat little app that lets you transfer files wirelessly. Download and install this free app on your Kindle Fire, and when you run the app, once you identify the wi-fi network used by the Kindle Fire, you'll see a display giving you a web address that you can point a browser on any computer that's also on your network. The address will include a port number, similar to the following:

http://192.168.1.15:8000

Point your computer's web browser to the address you're given (yours will likely differ from this example) and you'll see a display like the following:

Wi-Fi File Explorer gives you a file explorer view of all the folders on your Kindle Fire HD. You can drill down into any folder, and use the Download button at the top of the Wi-Fi File Explorer window to move files from your home computer to your Kindle Fire, without the hassle of wires.

Chapter 6: Email Tips, Tricks, and Traps

One of the many capabilities of the Kindle Fire centers on the email client that is built into the device. All of the basic features that you would expect to find in an email client are here; you can open and read mail, reply to and compose mail, download attachments, and send email with attached files. Tips, tricks, and traps dealing with email are covered in this chapter.

Setting up your Kindle Fire HD E-mail

Set up an email account on your Kindle Fire. From the Home screen, tap Apps in the Navigation bar. When your Apps screen appears, touch 'On Device' at the upper right to see the apps on your device, then tap the Email app. Assuming you've never setup an email account on your Kindle Fire, the Add Accounts screen will appear, as shown here:

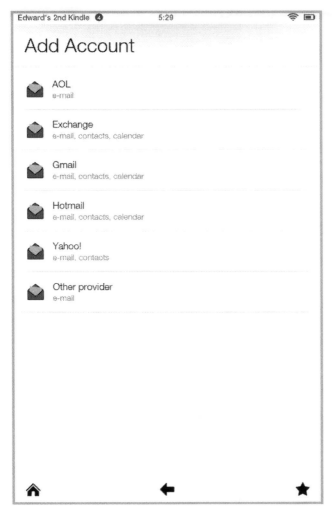

Select the type of account you want to add, and an Add Accounts screen will appear for that particular type of account. The following screen shows the Add Account screen for Gmail; however, all of the add accounts screens initially display the same screen, asking for your name, email address, password, and a description.

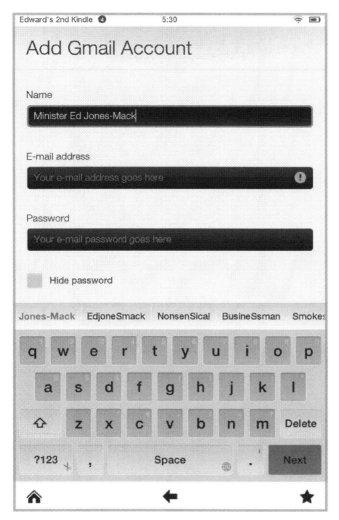

Enter this information, and your Kindle Fire will attempt to connect the new email account settings with the servers of your email account provider. Once it successfully does so, you'll see a synchronization options screen, similar to the one shown here:

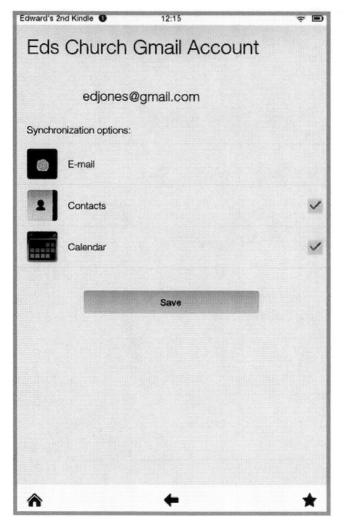

Eds Church Gmail Account

edjones@gmail.com

Synchronization options:

E-mail

Contacts   ✓

Calendar   ✓

Save

Under the default settings, your email is automatically synchronized. Choose whether you want your contacts and calendar synchronized for the same account, and if so, turn on the respective check boxes for these options, then click Save. Once the account has been set up, you can click the View Account button to open your mailbox.

Kindle Fire receives incoming emails, but is unable to send outgoing emails. After setup of an email account, some users report that they are able to receive emails, but can't send mail. The problem is usually that when you fill in the setup screen, the Kindle Fire assumes that your username is also your outgoing SMTP address setting. And this is true with most providers, but not with all providers. As an example, if your email provider is Comcast cable, and your full email address is *johndoe@comcast.net*, when going through the setup screen, you probably entered *johndoe* when prompted for a user name. As a result, the Kindle Fire's email client is trying to send out email with an SMTP address setting of *johndoe*, when the setting should be *johndoe@comcast.net*. To solve the problem, go back into the email settings you have on your Kindle Fire, and enter the entire outgoing email address manually.

Setting up E-mail with Microsoft Exchange

Create a Microsoft Exchange e-mail account on the Kindle Fire HD (if you are using Exchange). In the business world, one of the most commonly-used sources of e-mail is Microsoft's Exchange, a server-based messaging system used by thousands of companies and organizations worldwide. Exchange is offered both as a hardware-and-software based solution that is typically installed and managed by an organization's IT staff, or as a cloud-based solution (as is the case with Microsoft's Office 365, a subscription-based service offered by Microsoft). In either case, if Microsoft Exchange is the provider of e-mail, contacts, and calendaring at your office, the good news is that you can set up your Kindle Fire HD to access your e-mail, contacts, and calendar that are hosted by Microsoft Exchange. The not-so-good news is that the setup to do this is a

71

bit tricky, so we've detailed the steps you will need here. You'll want to turn on your Kindle Fire HD and ensure that you have an active Wi-Fi connection. Once this is done, you can perform the following steps to set up e-mail, contacts, and calendaring from Microsoft Exchange on your Kindle Fire HD:

From the Home screen, tap Apps, then tap the e-mail icon. If this is the first e-mail account you are setting up on your Kindle Fire, an Add Account page will appear. On this page, in the list of mail providers, tap Exchange. If you've previously set up one or more email accounts on your Kindle Fire, go to the menus, tap Settings (or tap 'More' on a 1st-gen Fire HD), and choose Applications > Email, Contacts, Calendars. At the next screen, tap Add Account, then tap Exchange. When you do this, an Add Exchange Account screen appears.

On the Add Exchange Account screen, under Name, enter your full name. Under E-mail address, enter your full email address. Under Password, enter your password, and tap Next. In the Description field, enter a description for the account, and tap Done.

An Exchange Server Settings screen will appear next, and you may notice that various settings have been filled in. Before you get too excited, note that these are example settings, virtually guaranteed *not* to work. You will need to change most of these settings.

In the Exchange server field, enter the name of your Exchange server. If you're connecting to a Microsoft cloud-based Office 365 email account, the Exchange server name will be `outlook.office365.com`. If you are using a web-hosted Exchange account provided by a web hosting service like 1and1 Internet or GoDaddy.com, your hosting provider will be able to provide you with this information. If you're not using Office 365 or a web-hosted Exchange account, contact the Exchange server administrator at your organization's I.T. department for the name of your Exchange server.

The Domain field will contain the word, 'Optional.' Leave this field empty.

Under Username, enter your full email address, and in the Password field, make sure your password is correct, then click Done.

You may or may not see another "Security settings options" screen, asking about secure connections (SSL) options. If this screen appears, check that the 'Use secure connection (SSL)' option is selected, and the 'Accept all SSL certificates' option is turned OFF. After checking these settings, click Next.

You may see a Remote security administration notice that reads, "The server <Your Exchange Server Name> requires that you allow it to remotely control some security features on your device. Do you want to finish setting up this account?" If this notice appears, tap OK.

Finally, you will see a screen bearing the descriptive name of your e-mail account, along with synchronization options for synchronizing your contacts and calendar on the Exchange server with the contacts and calendar on your Kindle Fire. Turn on the Contacts and Calendar checkboxes as desired, to specify whether or not you want to synchronize your contacts and calendar items between Microsoft Exchange and your Kindle Fire HD. After making your selections, tap Save. (Note that by default, your e-mail will be synchronized between the e-mail account on the Kindle Fire HD and the e-mail account under Microsoft Exchange; you cannot turn off e-mail synchronization.)

After tapping Save, a 'Setup complete!' screen appears, and you can tap View Inbox to access your Exchange-based email on your Kindle Fire HD.

Customize E-mail operations with various settings

Speed up your email performance by hiding images. If you receive a large amount of email that contains embedded images, display of your messages can be slowed by the presence of the images. You can turn off the display of embedded images by default. Pull down the Navigation bar, tap Settings, and under Applications, within the 'Amazon Applications' subcategory, tap 'Email, Contacts, Calendar.' At the next screen that appears, tap Email General Settings. (On a 1st-gen Fire HD, pull down the Navigation bar, tap 'More,' and go to Applications > at the Settings screen, tap My Account, then Manage Email, and tap Email General Settings. With either build of Kindle Fire HD, you will see a screen similar to the following:

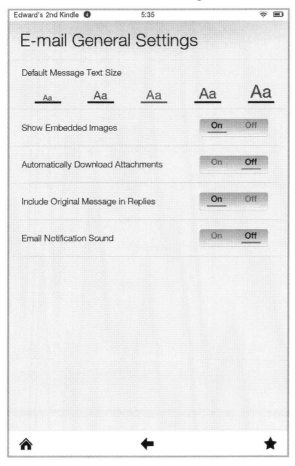

Show embedded images is normally on by default at this screen. Set this option to Off to speed up your mail performance.

Add a custom signature to save typing time. You can add a default signature line to the bottom of your outgoing messages, to save yourself the time involved in having to sign every letter that you compose. To do this, drag down the Navigation bar and tap Settings (or tap 'More' on a 1st-gen Fire HD), then at the Settings screen, tap My Account, then Manage Email, and tap Email General Settings. Select your email account, scroll down within the dialog box, tap Signature, and enter the desired personal signature.

Use Bulk delete to delete multiple messages. There is no need to delete messages one at a time if you want to delete a group of messages. Just turn on the checkboxes at the left of all of the unwanted messages, and tap the Delete icon at the top of the screen to delete the selected messages as a group.

Consider using an optional app as your Email client. While the Email client that is built into the Kindle Fire HD models does an acceptable job, you should be aware that this is not your only option for managing email. There are apps available from the Amazon AppStore, some of them free, that serve as perfectly acceptable alternatives to the Kindle Fire's built-in e-mail app. One that this author particularly likes is SkitM@il, by SkitApps.

SkitM@il is a full-featured e-mail client that supports multiple mailboxes on the Kindle Fire. If you are like many wired individuals, you probably have multiple mailboxes from different providers. Perhaps you have one address with Yahoo, another with Google's gmail, the third for a domain associated with your job, and a fourth associated with a cell phone carrier. Chances are, all your accounts support universal Internet mail protocol standards such as POP or IMAP. If that's the case, you can consolidate all your messages from multiple accounts into one place, with SkitM@il.

SkitM@il has everything you'd expect in a full featured e-mail client; automatic e-mail push (meaning, incoming e-mail messages appear in SkitM@il as they are received), access to synchronized messages when you are offline, and multiple folders for synchronization. From the main screen, all your e-mail accounts appear under the names that you create for them. Once you've added a new e-mail account, all of the folders associated with that account-- all mail, drafts, sent mail, and trash-- become accessible. Besides all the usual features found in an e-mail client (compose new messages, reply, forward, and delete), you can also move messages into folders, and "star" the messages for later review when you are offline. SkitM@il also lets you sort your mail in a number of different ways. You can sort your mail by date, by subjects, by sender, or by attachment type.

SkitM@il 's display is also highly customizable, which is a big plus over the default mail client that comes with the Kindle Fire. You can change the default font size and the styles used to suit your tastes. SkitM@il is simple to install, setup, and use; it supports POP, IMAP, and Microsoft Exchange (with WebDAV); and it stands a cut above the default e-mail that comes with the Kindle Fire just in terms of its flexibility.

Chapter 7: Multimedia Tips, Tricks, and Traps

One of the major strengths of the Kindle Fire centers on its impressive multimedia capabilities. Designed to provide you with a better multimedia experience, the Kindle Fire HD is small enough to hold in your hand, yet delivers a vibrant viewing experience with over 16 million colors on its high definition screen. The sharp, beautiful color display is backed by dual stereo speakers built into the device, along with support for Dolby sound. For the technically inclined, the Kindle Fire HD supports 3gp and mp4 video formats, H264 video encoding, with an 800 by 480 resolution and a 2500 kps bit rate. On the audio side, the Kindle Fire HP supports AAC, MP3, MIDI, OGG, and WAV formats, and uses AAC for audio encoding of movies' audio tracks.

Playing personal videos on your Kindle Fire HD

 **Play your personal videos on your Kindle Fire**. You can transfer video files or download video files and play them on your Kindle Fire. You cannot place them in the video library, but you can copy your personal videos into the /Pictures subfolder of your Fire HD (and no, "/Pictures" is not a misprint). Your videos will appear alongside your photos when you tap Photos on the Navigation bar. The only visual difference between your photos and your videos will be the presence of an arrow within a circle, like this:

which acts as a "Play" button for the video player. Tap the arrow, and your video will begin playing on your Kindle Fire HD's screen.

On a first-generation Kindle Fire HD, there is a default app for playing your videos. At the Home screen, tap Apps to display all of your apps. The icon for the Personal Videos player looks like this:

You can copy files that are stored in the 3GP or MP4 video format into the /Pictures folder that appears in the directory of folders shown on your computer when the Kindle Fire is connected by means of the USB cable. When you connect the Kindle Fire to the micro USB side of the charging cable and connect the standard USB side of the cable to your computers USB port, the Kindle Fire appears on your computer's File Explorer or file management system as a USB flash drive, similar to the example shown in the following illustration.

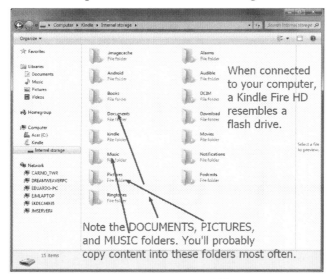

When connected to your computer, a Kindle Fire HD resembles a flash drive.

Note the DOCUMENTS, PICTURES, and MUSIC folders. You'll probably copy content into these folders most often.

You can then use standard cut / copy / paste or drag-and-drop procedures to copy the video file from the source folder that contains the video file on your hard drive to the destination folder that appears with all the other folders of your Kindle's internal storage under the device name 'Kindle.'

You can copy your photos, images, or personal video files into the /Pictures folder, and these will appear within a tiled directory style view when you tap Photos in the Navigation bar on your Home screen. In a similar fashion, you can copy .mp3 files into the /Music subfolder, and these will appear as songs when you tap Music in the Navigation bar. You can copy Microsoft Word documents, rich text format (.RTF) files, and text (.TXT) files into the /Documents folder, and these will appear when you tap Documents in the Navigation bar.

A file may exist in the acceptable file format of 3GP or MP4, yet may refuse to play on a Kindle Fire. Not only must the files be stored as a 3GP or MP4 format, the length by width (800 by 480) and video bitrate (2500) must fall within acceptable parameters, or the video will fail to play. You can use a conversion program on a desktop or laptop computer to convert video files such as your vacation movies shot with a DV camcorder to a format that will play on your Kindle Fire.

There is an excellent free, open source program for converting video files to the Kindle Fire format, and the program is available for the Windows PC, Apple Mac, and Ubuntu Linux machines. The program, Miro, can be downloaded at http://www.getmiro.com. The program may appear slightly complicated to use, at least initially. Fortunately, the getmiro.com website provides extensive documentation.

Import your iTunes/Zune Music Library to your Fire HD

Import your iTunes, Microsoft Zune, or other music library into your Kindle Fire using the Amazon Cloud Player. Amazon has an easy to use tool that makes importing your iTunes of other music library a simple matter. Open a browser window on your computer, and visit http://www.amazon.com/cloudplayer (if you are in North America) or visit http://www.amazon.co.uk/cloudplayer (if you are in the United Kingdom) and set up a CloudPlayer account. Once you set up an account, click the Import Music button at the upper left, and follow the directions that appear on the screen. After you've imported your songs into the Amazon Cloud Player, you can select any number of songs, click the download button, and download them to your Kindle Fire.

Downloading and playing YouTube videos

Download YouTube videos for later playback on your Kindle Fire. YouTube has long supported the H.264 video encoding format that is currently used by the Kindle Fire. And if a subject has ever been recorded on video, chances are that it can be found on YouTube, at least in partial, if not in complete form. YouTube is known for being the resource for millions of video clips. You don't even have to resort to using a PC or a Mac to download YouTube videos, because numerous YouTube video downloader apps are available for the Kindle Fire. A search of the Amazon app store for the phrase 'youtube downloader' will reveal a number of entries. One that has been tested by this author is the Droid Youtube Downloader by KastorSoft. The app is simple to use, it does what is expected of it, and it is free. (The app is ad supported, but the ads are small and fairly unobtrusive.)

Install the app, and its operation is simplicity itself. You launch the app, and a search box appears at the top of the screen. Type a search term, tap the magnifying glass, and the app will search the entire YouTube database for videos that match your search term. Find a desired video and tap the video, and another menu appears. From this menu, you can choose to preview the video, download the file as video, download the file as an MP3 audio file, or download the file as an AAC video file. Select Download as Video, and you will see a message indicating the percentage of progress saved, then a message indicating when the download is complete.

Once the YouTube video has completed downloading, go to your Apps screen and bring up your Personal Videos app. You will see an icon displaying the starting screen of the YouTube video, and you can tap the icon to play the video.

Storing pictures and personal videos in the Amazon CloudDrive

Under the heading of 'Where's My Data?, chapter 1 introduced the concept of cloud based storage, which greatly increases your possible maximum storage space by saving data to web servers that reside on the Internet. As far as multimedia goes, you can store your photos and personal videos in the cloud, on Amazon's CloudDrive, to be specific. If you tap the Photos option on the Navigation bar and you never set up a CloudDrive account at Amazon, you'll see a welcome screen like the following:

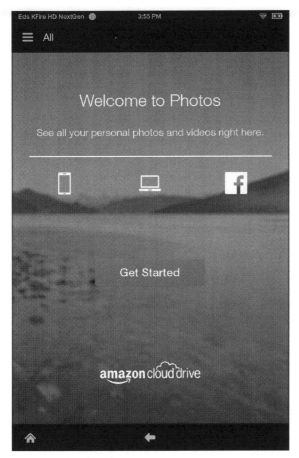

Click the Get Started link, and you will first be asked if you wish to send an app to your smartphone. (The app lets you view photos or videos stored in the Amazon cloud on your smartphone, or upload photos or videos from your phone to the Amazon cloud.) Confirm if you wish by clicking Yes and by entering your cell phone number where prompted.

Next, you will be asked if you want a link for the CloudDrive app sent to your PC. Click Yes if desired, and you will receive a link via e-mail that lets you download the Amazon CloudDrive app for your Windows or Apple IOS-based PC.

Once you've installed the app on a compatible smartphone or personal computer, you can move photos from your phone or your PC to Amazon's CloudDrive storage.

Viewing your CloudDrive photos on a Kindle Fire

After you've set up your CloudDrive account and uploaded any photos, just tap Photos in the Navigation bar on your Kindle Fire HD. Your photos will appear in a tile-based layout like that shown in the following illustration:

You can tap on any photo and it expands to fill your Kindle Fire HD's screen, like the example shown:

Press ↑ symbol to move up to tiled view of all photos.

Tap Delete to remove photo.

Tap Share icon to share photo via e-mail, Facebook, or Twitter.

You can also perform a long press (press and hold) on any photo in your collection, and a popup menu will appear. Your menu choices are Share, Edit, Info, Download, and Delete.

Share lets you share the photo, either by means of an e-mail account, or through Facebook or Twitter, if these are linked to your Kindle Fire HD by means of the social settings.

Edit launches the native Kindle Photo Editor that you can use to make basic changes to your photos. You can change the brightness or contrast, crop your photo, reduce red eye, apply filters, and apply other special effects.

Info displays digital information stored about the photo, including the filename, creation date, dimensions (in pixels), and file size.

Download downloads the photo onto your device from the Amazon cloud, so that you will not need a Wi-Fi connection to display the photo.

Delete deletes the photo from your device.

The Amazon Cloud Storage account provides you with 5 GB of storage space, which is roughly enough to store over 2200 average photos. This amount of storage space would easily consume most of what is available on a Kindle Fire HD purchased with the standard 8 GB of memory. Since the Amazon CloudDrive account costs you nothing with a 5 GB allotment, it is well worth your taking the time to install and use the Amazon CloudDrive app.

Chapter 8: Camera Tips, Tricks, and Traps

IMPORTANT NOTE: This chapter does not apply to all current models of the Kindle Fire HD. As of early October 2013, the 7-inch screen models of the Kindle Fire HD do not feature a built-in camera.

One major difference between the first and second generation Fire HD 7-inch models is that the first generation builds featured a front facing digital camera. If you own a second-generation Fire HD with a 7-inch screen, you can ignore this chapter and skip to the chapter that follows.

For you first generation Fire HD owners (and owners of the 8.9-inch model from either generation), Amazon originally touted this camera for the purpose of making free video calls at home or abroad. The front-facing camera on the Kindle Fire HD can be used to take pictures using many of the camera applications available in the Amazon Appstore such as Photo Editor by Macgyver, Pythion's HD Camera Kindle Tablet Edition, Camera Fun Pro, PicSay Pro, and PicShop Lite, and you can use the camera for video chat with the Skype app, which comes pre-installed on the Fire HD. You can also use the Facebook app to take and share photos with Facebook friends.

When viewing the first-gen Fire HD with its off/on switch facing to the right, the camera is located within the small circle at the top center of the screen (see illustration). Both generations of the 8.9-inch Fire HD have a front-facing camera mounted in a similar fashion, at the top center of the screen side of the device.

Camera location

Off/On switch

The camera is a 1.3 megapixel camera, and there is no flash included, so don't expect great results under low lighting. The camera does perform adequately under average lighting conditions, and if you are using a camera app, you'll gain access to a number of user adjustable features that can enhance the quality of photos or videos. Since the camera is front facing, it's clear that Amazon designed it initially to support video chatting or video conferencing with apps such as the Skype app. But since the release of the first-gen Kindle Fire HD, a number of camera apps have become available that let you do much more with the built-in camera than just video chat, and that is the subject of this chapter.

Using the 1st-Gen. Kindle Fire's built-in Camera app

Take photos with the built-in camera app. When the Kindle Fire HD was first released, the camera could only be used by the preloaded Skype app, designed for use with video chatting. Since then, it must have become obvious to the design team at Amazon that people wanted to use the built in camera to simply take their own photos, because Amazon added a basic camera app with the release of version 7.2.2 of the operating system. If you've been online anytime recently with your Kindle Fire HD, the update will have taken place automatically. If you wish to check, pull down the Status bar on the top of the screen, tap More, under Settings tap Device, then tap About. Under System Version, you should see a value of 7.2.2 or higher. If you don't, click the Update Your Device button to the right.

You will probably want to add a camera app from the Amazon AppStore, because the built in camera app leaves much to be desired. The built in camera app is designed to take pictures of objects in a close in view such as faces, and there is no provision for filming a video. The built in app also lacks any provision for changing settings such as exposure time and light level. Still, if all you need is point and click simplicity for taking photos, the built in app will serve you.

To get to the built in camera app, swipe the shortcut bar to the far right, and tap Photos. At the next screen, you will see any photos you have taken. (If you have not taken any photos, you'll see an introductory screen for Amazon's Cloud Drive Photo storage feature.) At the upper right, you will also see a camera icon. Tap this icon, and you will be placed in camera mode.

At the center of one side (depending on your device's orientation), you'll see a shutter icon. Tap this icon, and the camera will take a photo and store the picture in your photos folder.

After taking pictures with the camera, you can tap once in the center of the screen, then tap the Back arrow once to move out of the camera app and into the display of your photos. You can now finger swipe left or right to view all of your photos.

Use Shortcuts to send, share, or delete photos. With any photos visible on your screen, tap once in the center of the screen to bring up a menu of shortcuts, as shown in the illustration.

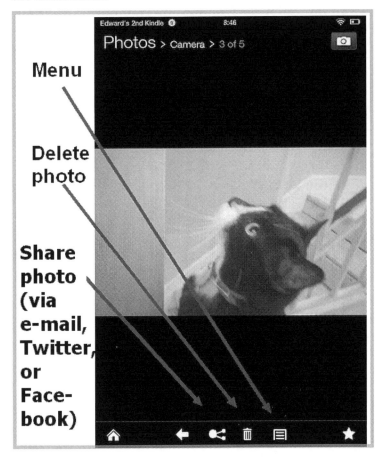

Tap the envelope icon to share your photo via Facebook or Twitter (if you've linked your Facebook or Twitter accounts to your Fire HD). You can also attach your photo to an email, and you can then compose the email and send it using the techniques described in this book's chapter on email. You can tap the trash can icon to delete the photo from your Kindle Fire, or you can tap the menu icon to reveal a menu with 3 choices: Send, Help, and Settings. The Send option brings up another menu that lets you choose to send the photo either via email, or to a shared location on the same network that is providing your wi-fi signal. The Help menu takes you to an online user guide that explains many of the same topics that this chapter is about: taking pictures, viewing your photos, and managing your photos.

You can quickly delete unwanted photos while viewing them. When any photo is visible, perform a long-press near the center of the photo. When a "Remove from device?" option appears, tap this option to delete the photo.

Adding capabilities with third-party camera apps

Use an Optional Camera App with the first-gen Fire HD for more capabilities. As mentioned earlier, if you plan to make any extensive use of the first-gen Fire HD's built in camera, you will want to download a camera app for your machine. Photo Editor by Macgyver is one good free app that lets you access the camera, and this app provides photo editing capabilities, as well. The app is ad supported, but the advertisements are so minor in size as to not get in the way of the use of the app. Additionally, there are a number of apps, reasonable in cost, that both let you take photos and videos using the built in camera of the Kindle Fire HD. One that I especially like is the HD Camera (Kindle Tablet Edition), by Python. The app is priced at $1.99 at the time of this writing, and two features alone make it well worth the small cost, in this author's opinion: a self timer, and support for video. One of the features missing from the Kindle Fire HD is a built-in support for video recording. Python's HD Camera (Kindle Tablet Edition) not only allows you to take pictures, it also lets the built in camera in the Kindle Fire HD record video. The video quality could best be described as fair; if you want high definition, you are not going to get it from the 1.3 megapixel camera built into the first-gen Kindle Fire HD, no matter what app you are using. Still, the result, both with video and with still photos, would be called "good enough" by many for everyday use.

If you install and launch Photo Editor by Macgyver, Python's HD Camera Kindle Tablet Edition, or one of the other optional apps designed to use the Kindle Fire's built in camera, you will see controls similar to those shown in the following illustration.

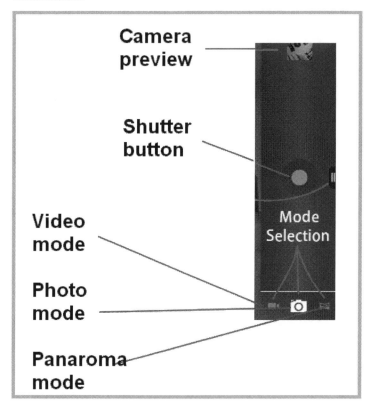

Pressing the large circular button will take a photo, and the small circle (if your app has one) can be finger-swiped to the left or to the right, or up and down, to increase or decrease the magnification factor (zoom). Most camera apps will cause the Fire HD's built in camera to start in the default photo taking mode, but note as shown in the illustration that there are also options for taking videos, and with some apps, for composing panoramic (or wide scene-based) shots.

Note that different apps may change the location of these camera controls. The location of the controls shown in the illustrations here are the locations used by both apps mentioned in this chapter (Photo Editor by Macgyver and Python's HD Camera Kindle Tablet Edition). If you choose to go with a different app, your control locations may differ, and you should refer to the documentation provided with the app to determine the precise location and nature of your camera's controls.

Changing your Camera Settings (When Necessary)

Use optional settings when necessary to enhance the quality of your photos. With both apps mentioned in this chapter, there are 3 settings that you can customize when using the camera photos. They are Scene mode, Exposure, and White Balance. (You can get to these settings by pressing a "Settings" icon or an "Options" icon, depending on the app that you are using.) Tap Scene Mode, and a menu appears with the following five settings: Auto, Action, Night, Sunset, and Party. In Auto, the camera takes its best guess based on general light levels. Action is designed to take photos of fast moving objects, Party adjusts the exposure to compensate for indoor low level light shots, Sunset is designed for sunset photos, and Night sets the exposure for photos taken at night.

Exposure is normally set to zero, a value midway between the maximum and minimum values. If you want to increase the light in your photo, use a positive value, and to decrease the light in the photo, use a negative value. The default of 0 works best for most conditions, but you can experiment to find the best value for your photos.

If your app has a self-timer feature, use it to make photos of group shots easy. If you opt for the HD camera Kindle tablet edition as your optional camera app, there is a self timer feature that makes it much easier to take pictures of groups of people, even with the front-facing camera built into the first-gen Fire HD. When you first open the app, tap Timer Cam, then tap the delay icon at the lower right to choose a 10 second delay, a 5 second delay, or no delay. You can then tap the circular icon at the center right to start the timer and take the photo after the delay period has completed its countdown to zero.

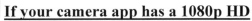 **If your camera app has a 1080p HD setting, do NOT try to use it!** Some apps, including the HD Camera (Kindle Fire Edition) have a 1080 pixel setting within their video settings. This setting exists because these apps are written to run on other Android devices, many of which are based on hardware supporting the 1080 pixel HD resolution (such as the Kindle Fire HDX 8.9-inch model with rear-facing high-definition camera). The first-gen Fire HD does *not* support this resolution, and if you select such an option, the app will probably crash and you may have to restart your Kindle Fire. (While the Fire HD's display may qualify as high-definition, the built-in camera does not.) If the app that you are using has an option for resolution settings, avoid any settings higher than 720 pixels.

When filming video, turn the camera "upside down." If you are using an app that supports video filming, you'll likely find that the Fire HD gives proper results when the built-in camera is facing downwards, and not at the top of the device. (This behavior doesn't appear to affect all apps that support video, but it does appear to affect many apps, so you may want to check the operation of your chosen app before attempting to record that all-important wedding or graduation using your Kindle Fire HD.)

Getting photos from your Fire HD to your computer

Copy photos from your Kindle Fire directly to your computer. One way to move photos from your Kindle Fire to your computer is to send the photos by e-mail, but there's another method that is often faster, especially when you have a large number of photos. You can transfer photos from your Kindle Fire to your computer using the following steps. First, connect the Kindle Fire to the computer using the USB cable. Open the Computer folder on your computer. (If you are running Windows, you can go to the Start menu and select Computer.) Open the Computer folder and select Kindle, then open that folder and select the Internal Storage folder. Open the Internal Storage folder and look for a folder named DCIM.

Open the DCIM folder and look for a folder named Camera. Open the Camera folder, and you will see your photos taken with the camera. Select the photos that you want to transfer to your computer, then right click and select Cut from the menu that appears if you want to move the photos from your Kindle, or select Copy from the menu that appears if you want to keep a copy of the photos on your Kindle. Finally, navigate to the folder on your computer where you want to place your photos, then right click and select Paste.

If you can't find your photos, try a reset. At times, the Kindle's MediaScanner service does not see new pictures immediately. In order for photos and videos to show up, they have to be scanned and indexed by the MediaScanner service that is a part of the operating system running on the Fire HD. If you wait long enough, they will eventually show up, but you can force them to appear by simply restarting your Kindle Fire HD.

Chapter 9: Apps Tips, Tricks, and Traps

In this chapter, we look at the power of apps to add significant features and capabilities to your Kindle Fire. The tablet would be impressive if it were only used for reading books and magazines, for watching movies and TV shows, and for web browsing. But with a range of apps available from the Amazon AppStore, you can transform your Kindle Fire in an unlimited number of ways. Using apps, you can literally transform your Kindle Fire into a news or weather information center, a sports scoreboard, an international language translator, a customized radio station, a medical adviser, or a personal butler that reminds you of every appointment on your busy daily schedule. And of course, you can use an app to make your Kindle Fire into a game platform, so that you can play a few rounds of Angry Birds. This chapter will first detail various tips, tricks, and traps for apps in general, in a section we like to call 'Apps 101.' We will follow that with a listing of twenty apps that we feel that no Kindle Fire should be without.

About Apps

Apps for your Kindle Fire (or for any tablet computer, for that matter) are actually computer programs, engineered to handle a specific task. As such, they must be *installed* on your Kindle Fire, which is a sophisticated computer in its own right. You install apps on your Kindle Fire by first purchasing the app (even if it's free) from the Amazon AppStore. You then install the app on your Kindle Fire by pressing the 'Download' button that appears once you purchase the app. After the app has been downloaded to your Kindle Fire, the download button changes to display the word 'Open', and you can press the Open button to start the app. Once the app exists on your Kindle Fire, you can get to it at any time, by choosing Apps from the Home screen, and locating and pressing on the icon for the particular app.

Find and install the app you want. At the Home screen, tap Apps, then at the upper right, tap Store. When the main screen of the Amazon AppStore appears, tap in the Search AppStore box at the top of the screen. The box will expand, and the keyboard will appear within the lower portion of the screen. Enter a search term to bring up one or more apps matching your search term, then tap the icon for the app that you are looking for.

Can I run generic android apps that don't come from the Amazon AppStore?

The short answer to the above question is an unqualified "maybe," but it's also a topic that is far beyond the scope of this book. You may be aware of the fact that your Kindle Fire runs a modified version of the popular Android operating system originally developed by Google. And you may be aware of the existence of android apps from other sources on the web (such as Google's own Play Store). While it is possible to run some of these apps on a Kindle Fire, it takes some tinkering with settings, and it's not a practice that Amazon recommends. Nevertheless, if you are interested in pursuing this topic further, you are definitely moving into "geek" territory. As an accomplished geek, my recommendation is that (1) you tread very carefully when journeying into this area and (2) you refer to a "geek" level treatment of the topic. You can perform a Google search on the phrase, 'how to install playstore the Kindle Fire,' and a number of articles will appear in response to the search. Some will be well-written, and others will make you regret having ever asked the question to begin with.

Deleting Apps

There will be times you'll want to delete an app, perhaps because it's not what you expected, or it is a game you've outgrown, or something better comes along. Apps are stored in two places: in your cloud storage on Amazon's servers, and on your Kindle Fire itself. When you initially purchase an app (even free apps are purchased, you just aren't charged for these), the app is stored in your personal space in the Amazon Cloud, where the app is not taking up any space on your Kindle Fire. When you press the download button that appears on the apps' icon in the cloud, it gets downloaded to the memory space of your Kindle Fire itself.

Remove unwanted apps from your Kindle Fire. You can remove any app from the Kindle Fire by performing a "long press" on the apps icon, and choosing 'Remove from Device' from the popup menu that appears. The long press simply means that you press and hold your finger on the icon for a few seconds. At the Home screen, press Apps to display your apps screen. When the apps screen appears, select 'Device' near the top center of the screen, to display all the apps currently stored on your Kindle Fire.

Press and hold your finger on the icon of the unwanted app until a menu appears, then select 'Remove from Device' from the menu. This action will delete the app from your Kindle's memory space.

An app that's deleted from your Kindle Fire can still be taking up space in your cloud. Keep in mind that deleting an app from your Kindle Fire itself does not remove the app from your storage in the Amazon Cloud. If you want to delete the app from cloud storage as well, go to your Home screen, tap Apps, and then tap 'Cloud' near the top center of the screen. This will reveal all your apps that are stored in the Amazon Cloud.

Locate the unwanted app, and press and hold your finger on the app icon until a popup menu appears, then choose 'Remove from Cloud' from the menu. *Note that deleting an app from your cloud storage at Amazon also wipes away any subscription information you may have saved in the app, so you should do this only if you are certain that you do not want to use the app in the future.*

Troubleshooting Apps

As mentioned earlier, apps are computer programs. And like all computer programs, they will at times fail to operate as promised, misbehave, or go absolutely haywire. When an app fails to operate as expected, your steps in resolving the issue will vary greatly depending on what type of behavior the app exhibited in the first place. Some app failures fall into the 'hiccup' category, in which case it may be best to chalk it up to the "evil gods of operating systems" and to move on in life. Other failures can go beyond the level of major annoyance; as an example, a camera app for my Kindle Fire recently caused my Fire's sound to stop working in all applications, and the only fix was to perform a hard reboot and completely reset my Kindle Fire to factory settings. If an app misbehaves, crashes, or completely locks up your Kindle Fire, here are some procedures that you can try, ranging in ascending order from minor (meaning, 'let's hope this works') to major (meaning, 'lets hope you don't have to resort to this')-

1. *Close and restart the app.* Without subjecting you to a heavy dose of techno-babble, let's just say that Android-based computers tend to be more stable than some small computer operating systems (Windows, not that anyone is pointing fingers) because each Android app runs in something called *protected space*. From a programming point of view, each app can "play inside its own sandbox." This means that in theory, the abnormal operation of an app should not affect the entire operating system, nor should it have an effect on other apps. When an app misbehaves, the least troublesome step is to completely close the

app, then restart the app. If this does not fix the problem you can move on to-

2. ***Perform a soft reset on your Kindle Fire.*** This happens naturally whenever you power down the machine, so just try turning it off. Wait 10 seconds, and power the Kindle Fire back on, then try the app again. If the soft reset fails to bring your machine back to normal operation, you can resort to-

3. ***Perform a hard reset.*** With the Kindle powered up, press and hold the power button depressed until you see a "Shutdown Your Kindle?" prompt appear on the screen. Tap 'Yes' in response to this prompt, and your Kindle will shut down. Wait 10 seconds, and power your Kindle back up. You may notice a distinct difference in the appearance of the startup sequence this time, as the Amazon lettering "Kindle Fire" in white and orange will appear in the center of the screen, and will remain there for a short period of time (less than 2 minutes) while the machine restarts. Hopefully, this will fix the issue, because the most drastic step will also result in a definite loss of settings. But if you must resort to the most drastic step--

4. ***Reset your Kindle Fire to its default factory settings***. Be warned that if use this last resort, you will need to reset your username and e-mail account information that you've registered with Amazon into the device, and you will have to pull all your apps back down from the Amazon cloud (and reenter any user settings that may have been stored in these apps). To perform this ultimate reboot, use the following steps:

a. At the Home screen, tap and drag down from the top of the screen, and tap Settings. (On a 1st-gen Fire HD, tap and drag down from the top of the screen, and choose 'More' from the list of options.)

b. At the next screen, choose 'Device.'

c. At the next screen, choose 'Restore your device to Factory Settings.'

If your Kindle Fire still has operational issues after this type of reset, it is definitely time to get on the phone with Amazon Customer Service.

Twenty FREE Apps No Fire HD Should Be Without

As promised, here's a listing of 20 FREE apps (you heard correctly, the price is zero, nada, zilch) that this author believes should be on the carousel of every Kindle Fire. This is an admittedly subjective list, but all but one of these apps has also received a high average rating (between 4 and 5 stars) from Amazon reviewers. (The lone holdout, Facebook, earned a moderate 3 of 5 stars, but is listed based on popularity; after all, one-sixth of the planet is on Facebook.) And we've taken the time to include links back to the Amazon order pages for each of these apps. So if any of these apps suits your fancy, just click the title or the app's icon, and you will be taken to the Amazon page for that app, where you can click the 'Get App' button to download the app to your Kindle Fire.

Note that the write-ups of the 20 free apps that follow are excerpted from the publication, ***Top 300 (Plus) Free Apps for the Kindle Fire*** by this same author. If you would like to see the other 280-something recommendations detailed in that book, consider spending the reasonable sum of ninety-nine cents on ***Top 300 (Plus) Free Apps for the Kindle Fire*** by Edward Jones. (At the time of this writing, this publication is available only as a Kindle e-book. Using your Kindle Fire HD, search the Amazon store for ***Top 300 (Plus) Free Apps for the Kindle Fire by Edward Jones*** for additional details.)

Crackle

Crackle is an outstanding source of FREE (that's correct, as in 'no subscrber or pay-per-view fees imvolved) movies and TV shows. With the Crackle app installed on yor Kindle Fire, you get immediate access to thousands of full-length Hollywood movies and TV shows. At the time this was written, the lineup on Crackle included movies like Pineapple Express, Big Daddy, Joe Dirt, Mr. Deeds, Alien Hunter, The Deep, Panic Room, S.W.A.T., and hundreds of others. Also in the Crackle lineup are dozens of TV shows like Seinfeld, The Prisoner, Marvel Comics' Iron Man animated series, All in the Family, and Chosen, just to name a few. Twenty new movies and TV episodes are added to the lineup each month, from genres that include action, anime, comedy, crime, horror, thrillers, and sci-fi. Crackle is truly free internet entertainment at its best, and unless you only purchased your Kindle Fire for reading, you shuld definitely have the Crackle app as one of your apps.

Netflix

The app may be free, but of course you'll need a Netflix subscription to actually watch any content. Given that fact, if you are a Netflix subscriber, you'll want the free Netflix app for your Kindle Fire. You can watch all of the same Netflix videos that you might see streamed to your laptop, and if you've got a Fire HD, you can enjoy that Dolby surround sound which comes across nicely with a good pair of headphones plugged into the Kindle. Log in with your NetFlix account, and you can get their usual unlimited shows and flicks on your Fire, and can even pick up where you left off on a show you'd started watching earlier on your TV set or other portable device. Of course, no movie-viewing app would be complete without having the Internet Movie Database (IMDb) app so you can get a good idea of what you're watching before you decide to watch it; the Internet Movie Database app is described next.

IMDb

  If you are a movie fan or a fan of regular TV shows, or even if you aren't but don't want to be embarrassed by those trivia-type TV actor questions that arise when you and your friends are debating "who played in what role," you'll want IMDb on your Fire. The app gives you access to a database of two million titles and four million cast members. It is divided into movies and TV sections, you can see what U.S. movies are getting the highest box office ratings, and you can even watch trailers for hundreds of thousands of movies. The app doesn't have anything that you couldn't get from the IMDb web site running on your laptop for desktop computer, but the interface is intuitive, the app is free, and it's easy to carry around on your Kindle Fire.

USA Today

From what multiple reviewers and this author say, the USA Today app for the Kindle Fire is the kind of app that every newspaper app should be. The content is beautiful, optimized to take advantage of the Fire's larger screen. Unlike many newspaper apps for Android-based tablets, the content is all free on this one; there are no subscription services to pay whatsoever. While you're online, the app feeds you constant updates, making sure you've received the latest news and information, and you can pull down stories for offline reading when you don't have Internet access.

The organization is logical, the formatting is colorful, and from a user friendliness standpoint it's a cinch to navigate. There is a wonderfully-intuitive 'swipe to the left or right' action within the main content viewer that automatically jumps you between stories in the smaller Articles window on the left, or you can tap any story within the Articles window to bring up the corresponding story on the right. Stories are laced with top-notch photography and occasionally with vivid video narratives. As an online newspaper, this implementation absolutely rocks. Oh, and did we mention that it's free? As a newspaper, USA Today on the Kindle Fire deserves five stars.

The Weather Channel

For the kind of in-depth weather reporting that you've come to rely on, you no longer need to turn to a cable or satellite TV channel. The Weather Channel is now no further than your Kindle Fire. Get animated and customizable radar maps; immediate, 36-hour, and ten day forecasts; severe weather alerts for the US and Europe; the ability to save multiple locations; and a "find me" feature that provides you with pinpoint local weather, based on your GPS location. Even the local pollen counts, which are often omitted from other sources, can be found at The Weather Channel. One particularly nice feature is the ability to touch a 'Video' button and get the local forecast for your area on demand from one of the TV anchors for The Weather Channel.

ESPN ScoreCenter

When it comes time to talk sports around the office water cooler on a Monday morning, you'll never be stumped for a score again if you install the ESPN ScoreCenter app on your Kindle Fire. You'll get scores, team standings, and news from hundreds of sports leagues worldwide. The variety of sports provided by ESPN ScoreCenter is just short of breathtaking- you'll find NFL and college football, NBA and college basketball, Major League Baseball, NHL Ice Hockey, and most other NCAA sports. If you are a big soccer fan, you'll find coverage of the Premier League, UEFA Champions League, the World Cup, and hundreds of additional soccer leagues and tournaments. NASCAR and Indy racing fans will find full coverage of motor sports, and golf, tennis, rugby, and cricket fans are all covered as well. If you are looking to keep up with the sports scene, you'll find it all in the ESPN ScoreCenter app.

Facebook by Facebook

This is the Facebook app for the Kindle Fire, engineered by the programmers at Facebook. It's basically the same app that was created by Facebook for generic Android-based tablets, with a few tweaks in the programming code to allow it to run under the heavily modified version of the Android operating system used by the Kindle Fire.

If you are familiar with Facebook, you have an idea of what to expect, and you do get these basics from the Facebook app. The news feed is here, and a new button at the upper right of the news feed quickly shows you who among your Facebook friends is available to message. When sending messages from within the app, you can see who is active, so you will have an idea as to when you can expect a reply. As with Facebook from the web, you can see what your friends are up to; share updates, photos, and videos; get notifications when others 'like' or comment on your posts; and text, chat, and carry on group conversations.

All that being said, the Facebook app gets a 'middle of the road' rating from Amazon reviewers, having had its fair share of teething problems. The most commonly experienced problem, according to numerous Amazon reviewers, is an inability to see more than roughly ten posts in your message wall or in the news feed. This problem has been reported to Facebook for about as long as the Facebook app has been in existence (which has been for some months now). If you install a Facebook app and you encounter the same type of behavior, you may want to uninstall the app and consider other ways to get to Facebook, one of which is mentioned in the paragraphs that follow.

Calculator Plus FREE by Digital Cherry, LLC

This app earned a listing in a "best free apps" article written by USA Today, and for good reason. Calculator Plus consistently earns five stars from reviewers, thanks to its intuitive interface, its feature set, and its ease of use. It is a simple calculator with just the basics, but those basics likely make for 98% of what most people need in a calculator. The app takes advantage of the Kindle Fire's large screen to present a very basic, but totally functional desktop style calculator. You get the basic keys (+), (-), (*), (/), and (%), along with a backspace key that works intuitively in concert with the calculator's multiline display, allowing you to use the backspace key to "undo" past operations. This free app is ad supported, but the ads are unobtrusive and nearly impossible to accidentally hit while using the calculator function keys.

PageOnce Money and Bills by PageOnce Corp.

CNN/Money Magazine referred to this app as "the Cadillac of money management apps," and for good reason. You can use it to organize and track your basic spending, cash on hand, bills, credit cards, and the amount of money you have placed in investments. You can keep a high-level view of what you are spending, and even pay all your bills from one location (although note that to use the bill paying feature, the app has to connect with the PageOnce servers and there is a $.30 per transaction processing fee). PageOnce Money and Bills was designed to be a one-stop money-management destination. The app also helps you break down how much of your money goes toward different types of bills each month, from credit card bills to insurance bills to utilities. You will need to enter login information for your financial accounts, but the app has been certified by TRUSTe and VeriSign, so it meets high standards for mobile security.

Checkbook

by Digital Life Solutions

When you don't need all the features of a full fledged financial analysis or personal finance program, when all you want to do is balance your checkbook, there's Checkbook. This free app won't help you with money market rates nor will it make loan analysis evaluations for you, but it will do a first class job of helping you balance as many ledger accounts, checking or savings, as you wish. You can set up multiple accounts, and you can transfer amounts between accounts, and Checkbook will keep track of your running balances. You can also choose to base your account on any one of seven different currencies. You can group transactions into over 30 different transaction categories such as mortgage, rent, groceries, car payments, insurance, and so on, and you can create your own custom categories. You can also set up scheduled transactions, so that these are automatically deducted from your account. You'll find it much easier to avoid those nasty bank overdraft charges with Checkbook running on your Kindle Fire.

HotelTonight

by HotelTonight

How often have you found yourself on a trip and suddenly due to a change of plans, you need a great deal on a hotel room? Or perhaps you're partying with friends, or a drive home is taking longer than you thought and you're tired, or you're stuck late at work and just don't want to make the drive home. Whatever the reason, HotelTonight is a great app that offers last minute pricing on a variety of hotel rooms. The deals are based on the known fact that hotels often have unused rooms that they are willing to fill at the last minute for rock bottom prices. It's worth noting that's the app gets its updates on deals from its database daily at noon in whatever time zone you're searching in. So if you're looking for a great deal on a last minute hotel room, you won't see that days' deals until after 12 noon.

Kayak

by Kayak Software Corporation

Kayak is a great multi purpose travel app for your Kindle Fire that lets you search for and discover flights, hotels, and car rentals, compare prices, and even get notification of cancellations and delays and gate information for your flights. You can also access maps of restaurants and ATMs in different locations where you are travelling. If you're in need of a last minute hotel room, or worried about a gate change or a flight delayed due to weather conditions, or need a car rental or you would just like to see a map of the airport where you're making a connection, you can now do all of this in one single app, Kayak. One caveat is that the app appears to only use Hertz as a car rental source, but otherwise, this is a great app for all things travel related.

CruiseFinder

by iCruise.com

If you are a fan of cruising, this is one app that you'll want to have on your Kindle Fire. Cruise Finder is a comprehensive cruise vacation planning app that gives you extensive information concerning over 200 ships sailing with 20 different cruise lines. You'll find thousands of itineraries complete with day by day descriptions and route maps, online pricing, availability, and booking, photos of ports, stateroom descriptions and deck plans, and even parking and map information for cruise line ports. A 'Hot Cruise Deals' section keeps you up to date with last minute pricing, and a 'My Favorites' section lets you save your favorite ships, itineraries, and cruise lines.

YP Local Search and Gas Prices (Kindle tablet edition)

by YP

When your travel is more of the local variety, out and around your own hometown, the people behind the yellow pages have brought you a great little free app called YP Local Search and Gas Prices. You can search through over 16,000,000 businesses divided into major categories like restaurants, bars, hotels, doctors, dentists, mechanics, and more. You can check out the menus from over 300,000 restaurants, and you can find the gas stations that have the best gas prices in town. You can personalize your version of the app so that it is gives you fast access to nearby businesses, restaurants, and events in your town, and you can provide your own feedback by rating local businesses (you'll need to be online to enter ratings). If you live in an area of the country where gas prices can vary wildly from one neighborhood to another, this app can be worth having just for the possible savings in gas prices alone.

Adobe Reader by Adobe Systems

If you spend a fair amount of time working with documents that are in the portable document format (pdf) pioneered by Adobe, you may as well opt for the Adobe Reader as an app on your Kindle Fire. While you can open a PDF file in the default Kindle viewer, the Adobe Reader offers more features in terms of working with PDF documents. You can make the print larger or smaller at the touch of the magnification button. You can navigate in more ways, viewing documents in a single page format, or as a continuous series of pages. And you can search through a searchable pdf for a phrase, or e-mail a pdf as an attachment, things that you cannot do with the Kindle Fire's native viewer.

One feature that would have been nice to have would be a quick way to delete pdf documents from your Kindle Fire when you are done with them. That feature is sadly lacking from the Adobe Reader app for the Fire, so you will still need to manually go into your documents directory and delete unwanted files.

<u>iTranslate</u> by Sonico Mobile

iTranslate is a great free app that does language translation. If you're a student of languages or you do a lot of international travel, you'll definitely want to have this one on your Kindle Fire. The app does a magnificent job of combining voice recognition with voice output, so you can speak and see your language. The app will translate words, phrases, and entire sentences into any one of more than 50 languages. These words of one Amazon reviewer do a great job of describing the functionality of the program:

"I am fluent in several languages and was pretty impressed with this app. I tested with a realistic tourist phrase which was fairly complex "I would like to visit your best art museum. Can you give me a recommendation and how to get there."

I selected English from the left drop down list, typed in the phrase in English, and selected the second language from a drop down list on the right. I was impressed with the translation, the grammar was perfectly correct. Next to the text there was a button which pronounced the translation. The pronunciation was excellent and sounded like a native speaker. The intonations sounded "computer generated" but completely understandable. I tested Russian and Spanish." The reviewer goes on to state that "this was the first random sentence that came to mind, I did not try to find a phrase that would be translated well. I was quite impressed with the results."

iTranslate will even let you e-mail a translated message, share it via Twitter, or copy it into memory for use with another app. Supported languages (at the time of this writing) include the following: Afrikaans, Albanian, Arabic, Belarusian, Bulgarian, Catalan, Chinese Simplified, Chinese Traditional, Croatian, Czech, Danish, Dutch, English, Estonian, Finnish, French, Galician, German, Greek, Hebrew, Hindi, Hungarian, Icelandic, Indonesian, Italian, Irish, Japanese, Korean, Latvian, Lithuanian, Macedonian, Malay, Maltese, Norwegian, Persian, Polish, Portuguese, Romanian, Russian, Serbian, Slovak, Slovenian, Spanish, Swahili, Swedish, Tagalog, Thai, Turkish, Ukrainian, Vietnamese, Welsh, and Yiddish.

My Alarm Clock Free (by Apalon)

     My Alarm Clock Free is a straightforward, flexible alarm clock app that runs nicely in the background on your Kindle Fire, until it is time to do its job and wake you from sleep. There are a variety of built-in tunes that you can use as alarms, and there is also an option that lets you fall asleep to white noise, as well as support for multiple alarms. The alarm will sound even when the app isn't running, and a built-in dimming feature changes the screen brightness, to prevent unnecessary battery drain.

Inkpad Notepad for Notes (by Workpail)

When all you need is a digital notepad, Inkpad Notepad for Notes will fill the bill. It's not designed to categorize your ideas, nor build mini-spreadsheets nor organize your friends phone numbers into small databases; it just lets you take notes. It resembles a paper notepad, and you can jot down whenever notes you like. The note is automatically saved with a title that matches the first line in the note. Tap a 'Share' button at the bottom of the note to share the note via e-mail, or by sending an SMS text message to a cell phone.

WebMD by WebMD

In these recessionary times of spiraling health care costs and many underinsured due to circumstances often beyond one's control, it's great to have an app like WebMD. WebMD is the popular online medical reference library brought to app form on the Kindle Fire. Using the symptom checker feature, you can choose the body part that is troubling you, select your symptoms, and learn about potential conditions or issues. WebMD's exhaustive drugs and treatments database gives you information on drugs, supplements, and vitamins. A First Aid Essentials guide to medical emergencies is available offline, so whether you have a wi-fi connection or not, you'll still be able to access the treatment essentials outlined in the First Aid Essentials guide.

File Manager (by Appsolutely)

This great free app for the Kindle Fire lets you manage and browse files, open, delete, rename and move files, zip/unzip files, and send files via email. There are no banner ads and the app is completely free, based on the Open Source (Apache 2.0) License. A note of caution here: this app lets you see files that are normally hidden from your view on the Kindle Fire, and it's possible to wreak havoc if you don't know what you are doing.

Wi-Fi File Explorer by Dooblou

Assuming you have a home network with PCs attached to it, you don't necessarily have to resort to the annoyance of a cable connected between your Kindle Fire and your computer every time you want to move a file between the two. Wi-Fi File Explorer is a neat little app that lets you transfer files wirelessly. Download and install this free app on your Kindle Fire, and when you run the app, once you identify the wi-fi network used by the Kindle Fire, you'll see a display giving you a web address that you can point a browser on the computer that's also on your network. The address will include a port number, something similar to the following:

http://192.168.1.15:8000

Point your computer's web browser to the address you're given (yours will differ from this example) and you'll see a display like the following:

Wi-Fi File Explorer gives you a file explorer view of all the folders on your Kindle Fire HD. You can drill down into any folder, and use the Download button at the top of the Wi-Fi File Explorer window to move files from your laptop to your Kindle Fire, without the hassle of wires.

As mentioned earlier, the write-ups of the ten free apps described in this chapter were excerpted from the publication, *Top 300 (Plus) Free Apps for the Kindle Fire* by this same author. If you would like to see the other 281 recommendations detailed in that book, consider visiting the Kindle bookstore at Amazon, and spending the reasonable sum of ninety-nine cents on *Top 300 (Plus) Free Apps for the Kindle Fire by Edward Jones.*

Chapter 10: Printing from your Kindle Fire HD

      With all that a Kindle Fire can do (and if you've used various apps, you probably already noticed that it can do a lot), there's one shortcoming. Natively, there's no direct support for printing. You cannot just connect your Kindle Fire to a printer and print documents, emails, web pages, or other content. But with the right combination of apps and free services, you can print directly from your Kindle Fire. You can use Google Cloud Print, a free service that is linked to a Google account, to print to most wi-fi compatible printers. Once you set up Google Cloud Print to work with a wi-fi printer, you'll need an app like EasyPrint.

      First, get a Google account if you don't already have one, and set up Google Cloud Print using your Google account. You can find full instructions explaining how to do this at http://www.google.com/cloudprint. Google Cloud Print is a web-based technology that lets you print to wi-fi enabled printers via the internet. You can print to printers that are "cloud-ready," or printers that can connect directly to the internet without a connection to a computer. Using Google Cloud Print, you can also connect to older (so-called "classic") printers if they are connected to a Windows, Mac, or Linux computer with Internet access, and Google's Chrome web browser is installed and running on the computer.

Once you've set up your wi-fi equipped printer to work with Google Cloud Print, go to the Home screen of your Kindle Fire, tap Apps, tap Store, and search for EasyPrint. The app is free (it's advertiser supported, but the ads are sufficiently unobtrusive). After you download and install the app, you will need to tell EasyPrint your Google account username and password, and you will need to specify a default printer that all print jobs should be sent to. You can then use the menu bar options within EasyPrint to choose what is to be printed from your Kindle Fire. (The following illustration shows the EasyPrint app running on the author's Kindle Fire HD.)

You can choose documents stored on your Kindle Fire, pdf files, web pages, or documents stored on Google Drive under your Google account. As the illustration shows, you can also choose your Google accounts to be used with EasyPrint (you can have more than one Google account used by the app), you can view all print jobs sent to your printer using Google Cloud Print, and you can view the status of your cloud-based printers (if you have more than one printer registered with Google Cloud Print).

There are other apps available that will also let you print on your Kindle Fire using Google Cloud Print. Two that are free and work well are printer model specific; they are the Kodak Document Print App (works with Kodak printers), and the Hewlett Packard ePrint App (works with HP printers). If you happen to own a Kodak printer that is cloud ready, one nice feature of the Kodak app is that it also lets you assign an e-mail address (such as 'myprinter@kodakeprint.com') to your printer. Once you assign this address, you can send emails with or without attachments to the address from any device, not just from your Kindle Fire, and the e-mail plus any attachments will be printed on your Kodak printer.

If you've enabled two-step verification for added security on your Google account, you are likely to have issues getting EasyPrint or any of the Google Cloud Print-compatible apps to operate successfully on your Kindle Fire HD. This doesn't appear to be a limitation of the Kindle Fire; as of this writing, the author has been unable to use a Google account that has two-step verification enabled to operate with cloud printing from *any* device, including Google's own Nexus tablet. Your recommended option in this case is to set up a separate Google account, do not enable two-step verification on that account, and use the account solely for cloud printing.

Chapter 11: Security Tips, Tricks, and Traps

Amazon has managed to marry what is basically an Android-based tablet computer with the near-flawless customer service experience that makes for shopping with the company, and the result-- the Kindle Fire HD-- makes for a consumer experience that, in terms of ease of use, is hard to beat. That same design advantage, in the wrong hands, could be a major security risk. For that reason, this chapter provides some tips on securing your Kindle Fire.

Lock your Kindle Fire. An unlocked Kindle Fire is somewhat akin to an unlocked car with the keys left in the ignition. If you lose your Kindle Fire, or the device is stolen, whoever happens to "acquire" it could read your email, access your Facebook account, and possibly order a number of expensive items from Amazon by mail before you became aware of the loss. Make sure your Kindle Fire requires a login password to prevent unauthorized users from gaining access to the machine's content. At the Home screen, pull down the Navigation bar, and tap Settings at the upper-right (or tap 'More' on a 1st-gen Fire HD) to display the Settings list. Tap Security, then turn on "Lock Screen Password." Enter a password, then enter it a second time to confirm.

Make a note of your password in a secure location, if you are the type that forgets passwords. If you do lock down your Kindle Fire and you forget the password, the only way to restore operation of the device is to perform a default factory reset, which will also erase all of your existing settings and take the machine back to the factory "out of the box" condition.

Back up your machine's settings to the Amazon Cloud on a regular basis. You can easily backup your device settings simply by using the Sync feature on the Settings screen. Every so often (perhaps monthly), pull down the Navigation bar, tap Settings, and tap the Sync icon. Doing so will not only synchronize things such as your email and contacts, but also the general settings for the device will be backed up to your account in the Amazon Cloud. This way, if the device ever needs replacing, you will save a significant amount of time as you will be able to pull your settings from the Amazon Cloud down into the replacement device.

Restrict purchasing and browsing with Parental Controls. If you have young ones around the house that also use your Kindle Fire, may want to turn on parental controls to prevent young ones from surfing the web's more inappropriate locations, and to prevent their making unauthorized purchases as well. At the Home screen, pull down the Navigation bar, and tap Settings at the upper-right (or tap 'More' on a 1st-gen Fire HD) then tap Parental Controls. Change the option to ON, and enter a password twice to activate parental controls.

Hide your Fire's physical location, if desired. The Kindle Fire HD models equipped with 3G capability have built in GPS technology, and other models approximate your physical location using a type of tracking that depends on the unique Internet address (known as an I.P. address) used by your wi-fi connection. Some individuals do not like the idea of their computer telling the world where they are located, even if that location is a rough approximation. If you are the type of individual who prefers to keep your location private, you can turn off location based services. Pull down the Navigation bar, tap Settings (or tap 'More' on a 1st-gen Fire HD), then tap Location-Based Services and turn the option OFF.

Tip or Trap, you decide: **Restrict applications to Amazon apps**. By default, the Kindle Fire is set to only permit apps from the Amazon AppStore to be installed. There is an option under device settings to allow installation of apps from unknown sources. There are pros and cons to either choice, which is why I've listed this as a tip or a trap. On my Kindle Fire, I allow apps from other sources to be installed, but I'm an admitted geek. If you don't know what you are doing, or if you are not fully aware of the source of the apps that you download, you may want to leave this option turned off and stick with the Amazon AppStore for all your applications. (To change this option, pull down the Navigation bar and tap Settings at the upper-right (or tap 'More' on a 1st-gen Fire HD), then tap Applications, and change the 'Allow Apps from External Sources' to Yes or No, depending on your preference.)

Chapter 12: Battery and Power Tips, Tricks, and Traps

One of the many strong points of the Kindle Fire HD is its battery life. The seven inch HD is rated in excess of 10 hours between charges, and that's quite an engineering accomplishment given the Fire HD's bright, high definition screen. But for those times when you may spend hours and hours away from an electrical outlet, there are specific tips that can help you get more out of your Kindle Fire's battery life and go for longer periods of time between charges.

Dim the screen, lengthen the battery life. Much of the power consumed by your Kindle Fire goes toward lighting that high definition screen, and the brighter the screen is lit, the more power that gets consumed. So when you're seated in that cramped tin can called an airliner at 30,000 feet, flying across the Pacific, turn down the brightness. Tap once in the center of the screen and tap and drag down from the top then tap Settings (or tap 'More' on a 1ˢᵗ gen Fire HD) to open the Settings screen. Tap Sounds and Display, turn off Auto-Brightness, and move the slider for Display Brightness down to a level that's comfortable for reading. (Your battery will last longer, and you can always turn the brightness back up after you're at the hotel in Honolulu!)

Adjust your screen timeout. By default, your Kindle Fire automatically dims its screen after a certain period of inactivity. You can adjust the time period, and the shorter the period, the longer your battery life. Tap once in the center of the screen and tap and drag down from the top, then tap Settings to open the Settings screen, scroll down to Screen

Timeout, and set this to as short a time as you are comfortable with.

Shut down wi-fi when there's no chance of getting a wi-fi signal. In places where there is no chance of getting a working wi-fi signal (such as most commuter rail lines and most aircraft), the wireless circuitry inside your Kindle Fire HD doesn't know any better and stays unusually active, checking for a wi-fi signal and consuming an abnormally high amount of battery power. An easy way to prevent this is to switch to airplane mode, which disables the Fire's wi-fi. (You will still be able to access any content you've already downloaded, such as your books, music, most apps, and any personal videos that are stored on your device.) Tap once in the center of the screen and tap and drag down from the top to open the Settings menu, and tap Wireless. At the next screen, turn on Airplane Mode. (When you are back in range of a strong wi-fi signal, remember to turn off Airplane Mode).

Use earphones in place of the built in speakers. Most headphones and earphones use much less power than do the speakers are built into the Kindle Fire.

Every so often, run down the battery on purpose. If you're the type of individual that keeps your rechargeable devices connected to a wall outlet, you may actually be shortening your battery life in the long run. The type of battery used by the Kindle Fire (as is used by other tablets and most laptop computers) actually loses its effectiveness over time if it is constantly kept in a state of near-full charge. The way to prevent this is to perform what is called a "deep discharge"—you intentionally allow your battery to run down closer to the point of exhaustion before recharging your device. Doing this on a monthly basis will help keep your Kindle Fire's battery working near top-notch condition.

CONCLUSION

I truly hope that you enjoy using your Kindle Fire HD as much as I have enjoyed using mine and writing about the Kindle Fire. I do feel that Amazon's Kindle Fire is one awesome tablet, and as a technology writer I've got plenty to compare it to. In my household, there are two Kindles, a Barnes and Noble NOOK, a Samsung Galaxy Tab and a Google Nexus. (Did I mention that the Kindle Paperwhite and the newer Kindle Fire HDX are on order as I write this?) So many people think the Kindle Fire product line is just for reading books, checking e-mail and surfing the web, but the device can do so much more. Hopefully, after you have had the opportunity to try some of the many tips and tricks that have been outlined in this guide, you'll discover that for yourself.

-Ed Jones

To visit the author's Amazon page for a complete list of books, visit the following web site:

http://www.amazon.com/author/edwardjones_writer

Alternately, visit the author's website at www.getitdonebooks.com.

Made in the USA
Columbia, SC
08 October 2020